THE ESCAPE
AND SUICIDE OF

JOHN
WILKES
BOOTH

FINIS L. BATES

APPLEWOOD BOOKS
Carlisle, Massachusetts

The Escape and Suicide of John Wilkes Booth
was originally published in 1907

ISBN: 978-1-4290-1101-3

For a free copy of our current print catalog
featuring our bestselling books, write to:

APPLEWOOD BOOKS
P.O. Box 27
Carlisle, MA 01741

For more complete listings, visit us on the web at:
www.awb.com

Prepared for publishing by HP

F. L. BATES, Author.

THE ESCAPE AND SUICIDE

OF

JOHN WILKES BOOTH

OR THE FIRST TRUE ACCOUNT OF

LINCOLN'S ASSASSINATION

CONTAINING

A COMPLETE CONFESSION BY BOOTH

MANY YEARS AFTER THE CRIME

GIVING IN FULL DETAIL THE PLANS, PLOT AND INTRIGUE
OF THE CONSPIRATORS, AND THE TREACHERY
OF ANDREW JOHNSON, THEN VICE-PRESI-
DENT OF THE UNITED STATES

WRITTEN FOR THE CORRECTION OF HISTORY

BY

FINIS L. BATES

J. L. NICHOLS & COMPANY
MANUFACTURING PUBLISHERS
NAPERVILLE, ILL.   ATLANTA, GA.   MEMPHIS, TENN.

DEDICATION

To the Armies and Navies of the late Civil War, fought between the States of North America, from 1861 to 1865, this book is dedicated.

THE AUTHOR.

PREFACE

In the preparation of this book I have neither spared time or money, since I became satisfied that John Wilkes Booth was not killed, as has been supposed, at the Garrett home in Virginia, on the 26th day of April, 1865, and present this volume of collated facts, which I submit for the correction of history, respecting the assassination of President Abraham Lincoln, and the death or escape of John Wilkes Booth.

Personally, I know nothing of President Lincoln, and knew nothing of John Wilkes Booth until my meeting with John St. Helen, at my home in Texas, in the year 1872.

The picture which John St. Helen left with me for the future identification of himself in his true name and personality, was first identified by Gen. D. D. Dana, of Lubec, Maine, as John Wilkes Booth, January 17, 1898.

The second time by Junius Brutus Booth, the third, of Boston, Mass., (he being the oldest living nephew of John Wilkes Booth), on the 21st day of February, 1903, at Memphis, Tenn.

The third time by the late Joe Jefferson (the world's famous Rip Van Winkle), at Memphis,

Tennessee, on the 14th day of April, 1903, just thirty-eight years to a day from the date of the assassination of President Lincoln. I here make mention of this identification because of its importance. Among the personal acquaintances of John Wilkes Booth none would know him better than Mr. Jefferson, who was most closely associated with him for several years, both playing together on the same stage. I know of no man whose knowledge of Booth is more to be trusted, or whose words of identification will carry more weight to the world at large. While there are many other important personages equally to be relied upon that have identified his pictures there is none other so well known to the general public, having identified the picture taken of John St. Helen, in 1877, as being that of John Wilkes Booth—thus establishing the fact of actual physical proof that John Wilkes Booth was living in 1872, when I met him under the name of John St. Helen, as also when he had his picture taken and left with me in the late winter er early spring of 1878, twelve years after the assassination of President Lincoln.

It is well in this connection to call attention to other physical proofs of the identification of John Wilkes Booth by referring to the deformed right thumb, just where it joined the hand, and the mismatched brows, his right brow being arched and unlike the left. The deformity of the right thumb was caused by its having been crushed in the cogs of the machinery used for the hoisting of a stage curtain. The arched brow was caused by Booth being accidentally cut by McCullum with a saðre while they were at practice as the characters of Richard and Richmond, the point of McCullum's sword cutting a gash through the right brow, which had to be stitched up, and in healing became arched. And especially attention is called to the identity of these marks in his pictures. more particularly the one at the age of 64, taken of him while he was dead and lying in the morgue. During life Booth carried a small cane between the thumb and forefinger of the right hand to conceal that defect; observe this cane in his hand, in the picture of him at the age of 27. These physical marks on Booth's body settle without argument his identity. However, in all instances of investigation I have sought the highest sources of information and give the conclusive facts supported by physical monument and authentic record.

Wherefore, it is by this authority I state the verified truth with impartiality for the betterment of history, to the enlightment of the present and future generations of mankind, respecting the assassination of one of America's most universally beloved Presidents and the fate of his assassin.

FINIS L. BATES.

TABLE OF CONTENTS.

LIST OF ILLUSTRATIONS.

JOHN WILKES BOOTH.

Aged 27, Taken Just Before the Assassination of Lincoln, and Cane Which Was Carried to Conceal Deformed Thumb.

PRESIDENT ABRAHAM LINCOLN.
Holding the Proclamation of Emancipation, and the Log
Cabin Near Salem, Kentucky, Where He Was Born.

ABRAHAM LINCOLN, PRESIDENT OF THE UNITED STATES,

AND

JOHN WILKES BOOTH, THE ACTOR.

THE ASSASSINATION OF PRESIDENT LINCOLN BY JOHN WILKES BOOTH.

CHAPTER I.

LINCOLN—BOOTH

President Abraham Lincoln was born near Salem, Kentucky, United States of America, in a log cabin, on the 12th day of February, 1809, of humble parentage, and was president of the Northern Federal States of America, after the secession of the Southern States, beginning March 4th, 1861, whereby was brought about a temporary dissolution of the Union of the United States of America, when the political issues of the rights of States to withdraw and secede from the Union of States and the constitutional right slavery of the black race, as had been promulgated since, before and beginning with the independence of, and federation of the American Colonies; afterward transformed into sovereign State governments.

When, for the settlement of these issues appeal was had to the bloody arbitrament of battle, in the Civil War fought between the Federal States on the one side, with Abraham Lincoln as President and commander-in-chief of the Federal Army and Navy, with his site of government at Washington, D. C., and Jefferson Davis, President of the Southern seceded States, called the Confederate States of America, and commander-in-chief of the Army and Navy of the Southern Confederate States, with his site of government at the city of Richmond, and capital of the State of Virginia, situated approximately one hundred miles to the south from Washington City.

Mr. Lincoln was inaugurated President of the Federal States, at Washington, D. C., March 4th, 1861, and remained President until he received his mortal wound at the hands of his assassin, John Wilkes Booth, while seated with a party of friends in a private box attending Ford's Theater, in Washington, D. C., on the evening of the 14th day of April, 1865, and died from his wound on the early morning of April the 15th, 1865.

Mr. Lincoln was a lawyer pre-eminent in his profession, and had never associated himself with any church organization, and, in fact, was a deist, as also a firm believer in dreams, and to him they were presentiments forecasting coming events.

John Wilkes Booth was born near the city of Baltimore, on a farm, in the State of Maryland, in the year 1838, and was at the time of the assassination of President Lincoln about 27 years of age, and famous as an actor. He came from a family distinguished as actors and politicians in England as early as the sixteenth and seventeenth centuries, being descended from Burton Booth, the most popular actor with the English royalty known to history, and pronounced of all actors the greatest Macbeth the world has ever produced.

Henry Booth, Earl of Warrington, was his great-great-uncle, and John Wilkes, the Democratic reformer, in that he caused the extension of the franchise or right of ballot, to the common people of England, and who was at one time Lord Mayor of London, was his great-great-grandfather on his great-grandmother's side. While John Wilkes of England was distinguished for his great mental ability, he was equally distinguished for being the ugliest man in all England, while his wife was the most beautiful woman England had produced to her day.

3

John Wilkes Booth gets his name of John Wilkes from his great-great-grandfather, and his strikingly handsome personality from his great-great-grandmother. Thus it is said that John Wilkes Booth is given to the world from an ancestry known to England in their day as the Beauty and Beast.

John Wilkes Booth was a partisan in his sympathies for the success of the Southern Confederate States in the Civil War, bold and outspoken in his friendship for the South and his well wishes for the triumph of the Southern cause. In politics a Democrat, and by religion a Catholic, and a son of Junius Brutus Booth, the first, who was known to all men of his day as the master of the art of dramatic acting, being himself descended from the Booth family of actors in England, pre-eminently great as tragedians since the beginning of the sixteenth century.

CHAPTER II.

JOHN ST. HELEN

I have long hesitated to give to the world the true story of the plot first to kidnap and finally assassinate President Lincoln by John Wilkes Booth and others, as related to me in 1872, and at other times thereafter, by one then known to me as John St. Helen, but in truth and in fact, as afterward developed, John Wilkes Booth himself, in person telling this story more than seven years after the assassination of President Lincoln, and the supposed killing of Booth at the Garret home, in Virginia. Far removed from the scene of his crime, he told me the tale of his dastardly deed at Grandberry, Hood county, Texas, a then comparative frontier town of the great Western empire of these American States.

This story I could not accept as a fact without investigation, believing, as the world believed, that John Wilkes Booth had been killed at the Garret home in Virginia on or about the 26th day of April, 1865, by one Boston Corbett, connected with the Federal troops in pursuit of him, after he (Booth) had been passed through the Federal military lines which formed a complete cordon surrounding the City of Washington, D. C., on the night of and after the assassination of President Lincoln. But after many years of painstaking and exhaustive investigation, I am now unwillingly, and yet unanswerably, convinced that it is a fact that Booth was not killed, but made good his escape by the assistance of some of the officers of the Federal Army and government of the United States, located at Washington—traitors to President Lincoln, in whose keeping was his life—co-operating with Capt. Jett and Lieuts. Ruggles and Bainbridge, of the Confederate troops, belonging to the command of Col. J. S. Mosby, encamped at Bowling Green, Virginia. And the correctness of these statements, as well as to my convictions, the readers of this story must witness for or against the conclusion reached, for it is to the American people that I appeal that they shall hear the unalterable facts to the end that they may bear testimony with me to the civilized world that the death of America's martyred President, Lincoln, was not avenged, as we have been persuaded to believe, and that it remained the pleasure of the assassin to take his own life as how and when it best pleased him, conscious of his great individual crime and the nation's loss by the death of President Lincoln, the commission of which crime takes rank among the

epochs of time equaled only by the crucifixion of
Christ and the assassination of Caesar; in the con-
templation of which the physical man chills with in-
dignant emotions and the cold blood coursing his
viens makes numb the fingers recording the crime
that laid President Lincoln in the silent halls of
death and made Tad fatherless. But the truth will
be told, if needs be, with tremors and palsied hands,
in the triumph of right and the exposure of the
guilty ones whose crimes blacken history's page and
to associate their names through all coming centuries with Brutus, Marc Antony and Judas Iscariot,
if they are to be condemned in the story that is to be
told.

In the spring of 1872 I was entering the threshold
of manhood, a lawyer yet in my teens, in the active
practice of my profession, having settled at Grandberry, the county site of Hood county, in the State
of Texas, near the foothills of the Bosque mountains. Among my first clients in this locality was a
man who had been indicted by the grand jury of the
Federal Court, sitting at Tyler, Smith county, Texas,
for selling tobacco and whiskey at Glenrose Mills,
situated in Hood county, twenty miles to the southwest of Grandberry, who had failed first to obtain
a license, as required by the Federal statutes, as a
privilege for carrying on such business. The penalty

for the violation of this law being punishable as a misdemeanor by a fine and imprisonment, or either fine or imprisonment, at the discretion of the court. Hood county at this time was well out on the frontier of the State, and the country to within a few miles of Grandberry was frequently raided by the savage Comanche Indians.

Glenrose Mills was located immediately on the Bosque river, which flows at the base of the Bosque mountains, while at this point on the river was located a mill run by water power from the falls of the river, and on the bank of the river were located two or three small log houses, together with the old mill house constituting the buildings of the place called Glenrose Mills. One of these log houses was used as a storehouse by the man known to me as John St. Helen, which place, or house, however, for a year or so prior to St. Helen's occupancy had been occupied as a store by a merchant doing a general mercantile business, in a small way, carrying with his line of goods tobacco and whiskey for the retail trade, as did St. Helen in this place, as his successor in business at Glenrose Mills. The former merchant having removed from Glenrose Mills to Grandberry, opened up his business in the latter place before and continued his business in Grandberry after St. Helen had begun business at Glen-

8

rose. St. Helen occupied this log house not only as a store, but the back part of the same as living apartments for himself and a negro man servant, or porter, he having no family or known relatives or intimate friends within the time he was doing business at this house in Glenrose. For some reason unknown to me and my client, the merchant at Grandberry and former merchant at Glenrose had been indicted for having done business at Glenrose—selling tobacco and whiskey in the house occupied by St. Helen, in violation of the laws of the United States, as mentioned. This client had been arrested by the United States marshal and had given bond for his appearance at Tyler, Texas, to answer the United States government on a charge in two cases of selling tobacco and whiskey without first obtaining a privilege license, as required by law.

On ascertaining this state of facts, I sought St. Helen, with whom I had at this time only a casual acquaintance, and learned from him that he (St. Helen) was as a matter of fact doing business at Glenrose Mills, in the house formerly occupied by my client, the then merchant of Grandberry, who had been doing business at this stand, selling, among other articles of merchandise, tobacco and whiskey, and that he had done so without a license, as required by the government of the United States, and was so doing this business at the time, as alleged in the indictment against the Grandberry merchant, so that I insisted, as a means of protection to my client, that St. Helen should attend the Federal Court as a witness for the defendant, to testify to this state of facts, showing that the defendant merchant had been wrongfully indicted, confessedly so by St. Helen; who was at this time doing the very business of which my client was charged, without first having a license (for which my client had been indicted), and for which he was to stand trial in a short time before the Federal Court at Tyler. While St. Helen admitted his guilt and the innocence of my client, he declined to attend the court in any capacity on behalf of my client, without at this time giving to me any satisfactory reason as to why he would not do so, and when he was informed with more earnestness than was reasonably polite that any and all the known processes of the law of the Federal Court would be called into requisition to compel his attendance on the court, as he had been requested to do, and if need be witnesses would go before the Federal grand jury to have him indicted for the offense with which my client was wrongfully charged. St. Helen asked time to consider the matter, promising to act honorably in the affair, to the complete protection of the wronged man, conditioned

that he (St. Helen) should be protected from indictment and from any other process which would carry
him before the Federal Court. With this agreement we separated for the few intervening days
requested by him.

At this interview it was plainly to be seen that
St. Helen was sorely troubled and seemed to think
his final determination in the matter would be
fraught with the greatest consequences to himself,
much more, I thought, than was due to the apprehension of a possible conviction for the charges alleged against my client. But upon consideration
of the matter I was led to the conclusion that his
restless and uneasy manner was due to his long
outdoor life on the plains, and that by force of habit
he had acquired that restless and hunted, worried
expression constantly on his face, while the flashes
which came from his keen, penetrating black eyes
spoke of desperation and capacity for crime. All
this time his breath came hard, almost to a wheeze,
superinduced by excitement, or what seemed to be
a disease, possibly produced by exposure and bordering upon a bronchial or an asthmatic affliction
of the throat and chest. Thus looking and breath-
ing, with his body poised in easy, graceful attitude,
as if so by nature born, in his leave-taking to me he
raised his hand in slow and graceful manner, saying:

"As I agree, I shall see you, and of my purpose and destiny speak—until then———"

The words "until then," spoken with a soft voice and gentle tone, was a pleasant adieu, in fact, the entire sentence having been said, and I should say, dramatically acted in eloquence by word, motion of the body, jesticulation of the hand and utterance of the voice, not before or since equalled by any other person in my presence or experience. These expressions by word, voice and mannerism to me were food for thought, suggesting the inquiry whence came such a man? Who can this handsome man, this violent man, this soft-mannered man, this eloquent man, be? Unsuited to his vocation—the would-be merchant, in his log cabin store, and his life of seclusion in the wilds of the West. As in all things, came the day of final reckoning, and St. Helen walked into my office calling me to the private consultation room, turning and shutting the door, he said:

"I come redeeming my pledge, and have to say, first, that I desire to retain you as my attorney; that you may represent me in all matters of legal business concerning my affairs, and ask that you fix your reasonable retainer fee."

This I did, and when satisfactorily arranged St. Helen resumed his statement by saying:

12

"Now, that I have employed you and paid your retainer fee, you, as my lawyer, will and must keep secret such matters as I shall confide in you touching my legal interest and personal safety, and the prevention of my prosecution by the courts for the matters we are now considering or that might hereafter arise in consequence of your present employment, conditioned, of course, upon my making good to you the promises I have made."

To which I replied: "Yes. I understand."

"Well, then," continued St. Helen. "I say to you, as my attorney, that my true name is not John St. Helen, as you know me and suppose me to be, and for this reason I cannot afford to go to Tyler before the Federal Court, in fear that my true identity be discovered, as the Federal courts are more or less presided over in the South and officered by persons heretofore, as well as now, connected with the Federal Army and government, and the risk would be too great for me to take, and you will now understand why I have retained you as my counsel, and as such I ask that you take your client, indicted in the Federal Court at Tyler, and get him clear of this charge, of which he is certainly not guilty, using your best judgment in his behalf and for my protection. For this service I will pay your fee and all costs incident to the trial and trip."

13

Assenting to this, and accepting his suggestion as well as the employment by St. Helen, I set about fully planning the management of my client's case in the Federal Court with the purpose in view of a mutual protection of my client and John St. Helen. When after a few days of consultation and preparation my client and I were ready for the three or four days' drive by private conveyance from Grandberry to Tyler, St. Helen was notified and came promptly to my office the morning fixed for our leaving, and without further ceremony or discussion, handed me a large, long, red morocco pocketbook well filled with currency bills, saying that the amount it contained would be sufficient money for the trip, etc. The amount contained in this purse I never knew. Then, in complete readiness, my client and I, taking leave of our friends and thanking St. Helen, climbed into our buggy and were off for Tyler. After an uneventful trip we reached the hotel at Tyler on the afternoon of the third day out, to find the Federal Court in session, and after a night's rest I sought an interview with Col. Jack Evans, the then United States district attorney for the Eastern district of Texas, including Tyler, in Smith county. At this pleasant, courteous consultation an agreement was reached by which the government was to waive the presence of the defendant in court, who was yet at the hotel, ignorant of what was transpiring, and on the following morning after the convening of court I entered pleas of guilty, as prearranged with Col. Evans, when the court, Judge Roberts presiding, fined the defendant the usual fine in such cases and taxed him with the costs, amounting, as I now remember, to about sixty-five dollars in each case. The fine and costs were promptly paid by me from the funds provided by St. Helen, for which receipts were taken as vouchers.

After the close and settling of these cases I returned to the hotel and informed my grateful and surprised client of the happy culmination of his long-dreaded trial in the Federal Court for a crime of which he was not guilty. The processes of this court struck terror into the heart of the average frontiersman when their charges constituted a crime against the laws of the United States government.

I accepted the many marks of appreciation by word and act manifested by my client, which for the sake of personal allusion must be omitted. Suffice it to say, our purpose having been accomplished, our team was ordered, bills paid, as the beginning of the end of our stay in Tyler, and at the moment of our readiness re-entering our buggy, we were soon homeward bound full of hope for the future, made buoyant by success. While my thoughts and plans for all time were lined with rose-tinted clouds, the phantoms of vision, the treacherous shadows which light the pathway of all youth, but how too soon to be transformed to the black storm cloud of real life, flashing with the lightnings of despair, with low-muttering thunders, the signals of evils yet to come. But on we pushed, unmindful and careless of what the future should disclose, reaching Grandberry on the afternoon of the third day out from Tyler, when, with mutual good wishes and congratulations, my client and I separated to go to our homes, seeking the needed mental and physical rest from a trip the memory of which lives to mark an interesting event in my life and the foundation of a story in fact, the relation of which beggars fiction.

Then, just as twilight was being clasped into the folds of night by the stars of a cloudless sky, I sought seclusion while the world paused, lapped in the universal laws of rest, and entered dreamland on that bark of sleep, the sister ship of death, pillowed within the rainbow of hope, a fancy fed by the air castles of youth. Thus sleeping and thus waking the morning came, when I must needs take up the routine business of life again, and to learn much more of John St. Helen, who came into town. When he called at my office and I recounted to him the successful termination of the cases in the Federal

JOHN ST. HELEN.

Court at Tyler, St. Helen became profuse in his compliments and congratulations, when his pocketbook, which had previously contained approximately three or four hundred dollars, with its contents, less expenses and costs of said suits, was handed him. He took from it the necessary amount to pay the remainder of my fee. This having been done, St. Helen and I separated with at least seeming friendship welded by the bonds of mutual triumph; so that thus ended, for the present, the beginning of my acquaintance with John St. Helen, of whom I saw but little for the several months following.

CHAPTER III.

JOHN ST. HELEN LECTURES ROLAND REED

In the latter part of the June following my trip to Tyler, St. Helen came into my office and extended to me an invitation to attend, as the orator of the day, a barbecue to be given on the 4th of July at Glenrose Mills. Having accepted this invitation, in company with Gen. J. M. Taylor, made famous by his achievements in the Seminole Indian war in the State of Florida, and for many years an honored and useful citizen of the State of Texas, I attended this patriotic celebration. And I here make mention of Gen. J. M. Taylor as a tribute to his memory for the public services he has performed as well as his loyal friendship to me. And I in benedictions bespeak the repose of his soul in peace, long since left its tenement of clay.

Arriving at Glenrose on the forenoon of the day appointed, we were met by St. Helen, the master of ceremonies on this occasion, and taken to his private apartments in the log storehouse, which had been put in readiness for the royal reception accorded us.

With his servants in waiting all were attentive, while St. Helen entertained us with a lavish hand in princely welcome in that manner peculiarly his own. When I turned to view the platform and plot of ground made ready for the day, and the people as they were gathering from beyond the Bosque river, I saw the ideal location for the barbecue, within the shade of the wide-spreading water oaks in the narrow Bosque valley. And while thus taking in the situation, at the suggestion of Gen. Taylor, the General, St. Helen and myself left for the grounds. As we stepped upon the platform I was greatly surprised at the stage presence and consummate ease of manner and reassuring appearance of St. Helen, who was easily the center of attraction, and the commanding personality present. Gen. Taylor and I seated ourselves, while St. Helen remained standing. The people hurriedly gathered, giving us a hearty reception. Order being restored, St. Helen, posing gracefully, caused a hush of silence, and by a look of invitation called me to his side. Standing thus beside him to the front of the platform he, in his inimical manner, in his full, clear voice, with choice and eloquent language, introduced me as the first speaker, as he did subsequently introduce Gen. Taylor as the second speaker. On the close of the speeches made by Gen. Taylor and myself, St.

Helen, in a short, eloquent and timely speech, completely captivated the crowd, as well as ourselves, by his pre-eminent superiority over those with whom he came in contact during the day.

St. Helen's complete knowledge of elocution, ease and grace of person, together with his chaste and eloquent diction, seemed to be nature's gift rather than studied effort. It was but natural then that on the lips and in the minds of all present the inquiry should be, Who can this man St. Helen be? He being, in fact, a stranger to those present, who only casually knew him in this gathering, and without kith or kin so far as any one present knew, made the people more anxious to learn the identity of the man; an orator of the highest class, while the men and women lingered at Glenrose in the presence of St. Helen until the dying day cast its shadows upon Bosque's lofty tops and darkness was weaving the mantle of night over valleys below. Then congratulations, thank yous, glad to have met you and good byes were said.

At this parting Gen. Taylor and I left for our homes after a delightful day fraught with interest and events long to be pleasantly remembered by all in attendance, and to me it marked the beginning of a better knowledge of the character of and a closer personal relation with John St. Helen, whose physical beauty, so to speak, and mental attainments no man could fail to appreciate and no woman fail to admire.

St. Helen, the man who entertained you to mirth or to tears, as his own mood might inspire, while he himself stood unmoved by the emotions displayed around him—the man kind of disposition, careless of self, thoughtful of others, but living his own life in soliloquy, revelling in the thoughts of the master minds of the past. His selections and recitations were grandly and elegantly delivered, and despite your efforts your soul would be shaken and from the eyes tracing tears would steal like dew drops cast from a shaken reed. Painful? No. Unpleasant? No. But rather resembling a sorrow as a "mist resembles rain"—a sigh of hope, a tear of sympathy, or rather an exalted thought given expression to by a tear, the index to the feeling of the soul. St. Helen himself said he could not weep, though grief he knew to its bitterest depth, and lived a life bent with the burden of crime. These and kindred utterances made to me in private, in hours spent alone with him, aroused in me an anxious desire to know in very fact who he was. He told me his true name was not St. Helen, and the ascertaining of more definite information as to his true name was made unusually difficult by reason of his sensitiveness to the mention of all subjects pertaining to himself, in the various conversations had between St. Helen and myself before he removed with his business from Glenrose Mills to Grandberry, sometime in October following the 4th of July barbecue mentioned.

St. Helen's business did not seem to be a matter of necessity with him, as he at all times appeared to have more money than was warranted by his stock in trade, and he apparently took little interest in it and trusted at all times the waiting on of customers to his negro or Mexican porter, while he was in fact a man of leisure, spending most of his time after his removal to Grandberry in my office, reading and entertaining me after business hours, and in our idle moments in many other ways, but his favorite occupation was reading Shakespeare's plays, or rather reciting them as he alone could do. And his special preference seemed to be that of Richard III. and he began his recitations, as I now remember him, by somewhat transposing the introductory of Richard III., saying:

"I would I could laugh with those who laugh and weep with those who weep, wet my eyes with artificial tears and frame my face to all occasions——" following with much of the recitation of Richard III., as well as others of Shakespeare's plays.

While these recitations from Shakespeare charmed the ear and pleased all listeners, his rendition of Tennyson's Locksley Hall, once heard at an evening's entertainment, left an impress that years could never efface.

On other occasions I came in for lessons in elocution with full instructions and practical illustrations in minute details of when and how to enter upon the stage or public platform; St. Helen giving comical illustrations himself as to how the average statesmen come blundering on the platform, looking for a seat they could not find, finally falling into a chair apparently not of their choice but by accident, when they would cross their legs, stick the toes of their shoes inward while trying to hide their hands close down in their laps or behind their seats, or by clasping them in front of themselves and resting them on their crossed and agitated limbs, nervously rolling one thumb over the other, finally collapsing and wiping the perspiration from their faces with undue vigor and haste. All of which was impersonated by St. Helen in such a realistic manner that it was enjoyable to the extreme, as well as most profitable to me in after life. And as a result of this careful training I am now quick to observe the want of stage presence and lack of ease of manner in statesmen on the public platform or persons before the footlights.

23

St. Helen was not a man of classical education, but rather a born rhetorician and elocutionist, a learning apparently confined to and obtained from theatrical plays as well as a literature pertaining to the stage, evidenced by the many theatrical periodicals or papers to be found in his room. This intimacy with every detail of theatrical work was shown on the occasion of his criticism of Roland Reed, when St. Helen, Reed and I were alone together. Roland Reed in his boyhood was touring the country in his father's company, composed practically of Mr. and Mrs. Reed and their son, Roland, who was starring in light comedies by the impersonation of simple and frivolous characters, and they played two or three nights at Grandberry, which performances St. Helen and I attended together, and on the morning after the third night's play St. Helen requested Reed and myself to take a walk with him to view the Brazos river, which was then flowing with torrents of water. During this stroll St. Helen began with great earnestness to discuss theatrical subjects with Roland Reed, which discussion went into all essential details of the highest class of acting. St. Helen's criticism became personal to Reed, pointing out to him that in the impersonation of certain of the characters rendered by him, especially the character of an old maid, in which, as I remember St. Helen's criticism of Reed, was of the greatest personal severity, and among other things he said that in the character of the old maid Reed's acting reminded him of a simpleton attempting to impersonate the character and eccentricities of an idiot, more appropriate to the playgrounds of the innocent and half-witted than to the intelligent public before the footlights, and suggested that the artist should create the impression on his audience that the actor by his superior intelligence was creating and portraying the character of the foolish maiden, stamping the play with his individuality of character, and that acting the character in question without this was simply nonsense, which disgusted rather than pleased the intelligence of the ordinary attendant at the theater, etc.

Though this criticism was at times personal and severe, it was done with an earnestness that indicated that it was kindly given and was seemingly appreciated by Reed, for I am sure Reed profited by it in his after life, as witnessed by me in his improvement in his subsequent presentation of this character, which brought to my mind afresh the lecture given him by St. Helen. Could Reed have known, as I afterward knew, that this lecture given him was by John Wilkes Booth, what a surprise it would have been, and what an impression it would have made upon his young mind, and I am sure Reed would have esteemed the lecture a privilege. In fact, this lecture is a consideration which but few received at the hands of St. Helen—John Wilkes Booth.

After hearing this lecture and remembering what St. Helen had said to me, that his name was not in fact St. Helen, the former purpose of inquiry reasserted itself to know who this man was. Not only was he an orator, as I had found him at Glenrose, but again was he assaying the role of critic of high class acting, showing a knowledge, to my mind, of a born genius of high cultivation, demonstrating St. Helen to be a master of the art of which he was speaking.

CHAPTER IV.

ST. HELEN'S ILLNESS

Idle hours in the life of a resident of a small country town hang heavily and we are wont to find entertainment. Under these conditions St. Helen was at all leisure times as welcome as he was congenial, so that when he was not at my office I would spend my leisure time at his place of business. And now I recall to mind one occasion when I, in company with a mutual friend, stepped into St. Helen's place of business. Just as we entered I noticed several cowboys, as they are called in Texas parlance, because they herd cattle, standing at the counter eating and drinking, being waited on by the colored porter. St. Helen meeting us, stopped, as we walked in, standing at the entrance from the front and resting his right arm on the counter, when one of the boys turned, addressing him in a very familiar manner, saying:

"John, when you die the cowboys will build a monument to your memory."

St. Helen cast a look of indignation to the party addressing him, his flashing black eyes giving full

27

expression to his contempt for the proffered distinction of a monument by the cowboys. Then resting his thin, shapely right hand on the corner of the counter, standing in graceful poise, his head well poised, his beautiful black, curly hair flowing back from his high white forehead, holding his left hand well extended in gesticulation, said:

> "Come not when I am dead
> To shed thy tears around my head.
> Let the winds weep and the plover cry,
> But thou, oh, fool man, go by."

It was not so much what St. Helen said, but the manner of saying and acting it, and the voice by which it was said, that moved man to emotion, as would his recitation of almost any sentence that had in it a trace of sentiment.

The simple lines quoted will find but little lodgment in the soul of the casual reader, but when repeated by St. Helen, who could so beautifully portray each sentence in all of its meaning, it left its impress upon the memory of all who heard.

Five years after our acquaintance the hand of Time, with points of pain, began writing in deep lines on St. Helen's face the shadows of disease, the sign board on the pathway from the cradle to the grave. Emaciated, sick and weak, he took to his bed, confined in the back room of his store, where I and others, with the aid of a physician, gave him such attentions as his condition required. But despite our best efforts he continued to grow worse from day to day and both friends and physicians lost hope of his recovery. When I, tired and worn by my watch and continued attention at his bedside, sleeping and nursing in turn with others, was aroused about 10 o'clock one night and informed that I was wanted at the bedside of St. Helen, who was supposed to be in the last throes of death. On entering the room I found the physician holding St. Helen's wrist and counting his faint, infrequent pulse, which it seemed was beating his funeral dirge to the tomb. The doctor turned to me and said:

"St. Helen is dying and wishes to speak to you alone," and turning, withdrew from our presence.

I touched St. Helen, and after some effort aroused a faint response; he opened his eyes, which gave expression to that anxious and pleading look for help so often seen upon the face of a dying man when we are least powerful to assist. I requested to know of what service I could be to him. St. Helen, yet conscious, but so weak he could speak only in broken, whispered words, audible only by placing the ear close to his mouth, said:

ST. HELEN'S ILLNESS.

"I am dying. My name is John Wilkes Booth, and I am the assassin of President Lincoln. Get the picture of myself from under the pillow. I leave it with you for my future identification. Notify my brother Edwin Booth, of New York City."

He then closed his eyes in seeming rest. I reached forward and took from under the pillow a small picture taken of St. Helen a short while before his sickness, while on a visit to Glenrose Mills, by a photographer then tented at that place, as I was afterwards informed.

After getting the picture my attention was turned to giving St. Helen relief, if possible, not at the time thinking of his startling and important confession. I called the porter, and we began rubbing his entire body with strong brandy to give him vitality. He passed into a gentle sleep, and for a time we could not tell whether it would be the final sleep of death or a restful one, promising future consciousness and possible recovery. He lived through the night, much to our surprise and that of the doctor, who, after a careful examination of St. Helen's condition, was of the opinion that he was somewhat improved, but his condition continued extremely critical for several days, but the doctor finally announced that St. Helen's recovery was likely and in the course of a few days he was convalescent and by careful watching he was brought to final recovery. But it was many weeks before his health was recovered. After which our relations became more intimate and confidential, for St. Helen was a man who cherished gratitude.

We were alone one day in my office. I remarked to St. Helen that he had passed through a very severe spell of sickness and, in fact, we all thought he could not recover. To which he assented with a look of serious concern, and fixing his eyes on my face, asked:

"Do you remember anything I said to you when I was sick?" and waited with an anxious look for reply.

I said to him that I remembered many things which he had said to me.

When St. Helen said:

"Then you have my life in your keeping, but, thank God, as my attorney."

I replied: "Do you refer to what you said of your sweetheart and last love?"

St. Helen in reply said: "I have had a sweetheart, but no last love, and could not, in my wildest delirium have mentioned a subject so barren of concern to me. But your suggestion is a kind evasion of what I did say to you, which is of the greatest moment to me, and when I get well and feel like talking, and you like listening, I will tell you the story of my life and the history of the secrecy of my name."

"St. Helen, it will be interesting to me, at your convenience," I replied.

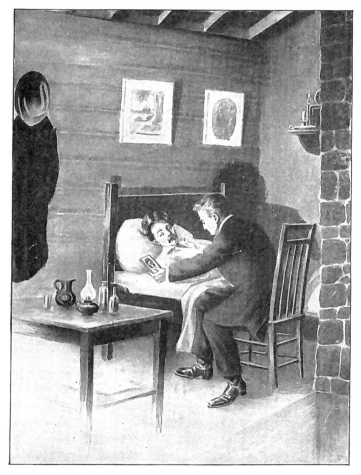

St. Helen Confessing the First Time to F. L. Bates That He
Is John Wilkes Booth.

Booth, Making a Full Confession of the Killing of Lincoln—
Accusing His Accomplices and Describing His Escape
to the Author.

CHAPTED V.

ST. HELEN'S IDENTITY REVEALED

After I had returned from an absence of several weeks, on professional business, St. Helen came to my office and invited me to walk with him to the open prairie. We went out about half a mile from town and seated ourselves on some rocks which had been placed in this open space under a large live oak tree as a physical monument of a land line or corner, a common custom at that time of marking located land lines. Seated upon this mounment we had an elevation comfortable and commanding the surrounding view. And St. Helen began his story by saying:

"I have told you that my name is not St. Helen, and, in fact, my name is John Wilkes Booth, a son of the late Junius Brutus Booth, Sr., the actor, and a brother of Junius Brutus Booth the second and Edwin Booth the actor."

At that time I think he mentioned a Dr. Booth as his brother, and two sisters whose names I cannot now recall from his statements at that time. That he was born on a farm in the State of Maryland, not far from Baltimore. That there was a young married woman taken into the Booth family, or the theatrical troupe of the elder Booth and known as Agnes Booth, an actress, but in fact she was not a Booth nor related to them, but was a Mrs. Agnes Perry, a Scandinavian lady, who was divorced from her husband and married some time in the sixties to Junius Brutus Booth the second. And St. Helen continued to relate many other family affairs, the publication of which would be to speak of the private concerns of the Booth family, which I deem unnecessary to make public. And while their relation in public would be no disparagement to the ancestry and relations of John Wilkes Booth, yet it-might be considered an abuse of confidence for me to do so.

St. Helen continuing, by reference to himself as Booth, said:

"I went on the stage at about the age of seventeen years, had succeeded and up to the beginning of the Civil War had accumulated about twenty thousand dollars in gold, which I had deposited in a bank (or banks) in Canada, owing to the uncertainty of monetary conditions in the United States at that time. I carried my money principally in checks of varying amounts to suit my convenience, issued by the banks carrying my accounts, which checks were readily cashable in the United States or foreign countries."

He said that his sympathies during the war were with the Southern cause, that he had become so enthusiastic in his loyalty to the South that he had to a great extent lost interest in matters of the stage and had given but little time and attention to his professional life or the study of the art of acting. That after the third year of the war, for many months prior to the 14th of April, 1865, he had determined that he could best serve the South's cause by kidnaping President Lincoln and delivering him over to the Confederate government at Richmond, Virginia, to be held as a hostage of war; that in preparation for the accomplishment of this purpose he had spent much of his time and money up to the death, as he called it, of President Lincoln.

At this point St. Helen grew passionate and full of sentiment, and after some hesitation, with much force of expression, said:

"I owe it to myself, most of all to my mother, possibly no less to my other relations and the good name of my family, as well as to the memory of Mrs. Surratt, who was hanged as a consequence of my crime, to make and leave behind me for history a full statement of this horrible affair. And I do desire, in fact, if it were possible, to make known to the world the purpose, as well as the motive, which actuated me in the commission of the crime against the life of President Lincoln. First of all I want to say I had no personal feeling against President Lincoln. I am not at heart an assassin. I am not a physical coward, or a mean man at heart, which the word assassin implies, but what I did was done on my part with purely patriotic motives, believing, as I did, and as I was persuaded at hat time, that the death of President Lincoln and the succession of Vice-President Johnson, a Southern man, to the presidency, was the then only hope for the protection of the South from misrule and the confiscation of the landed estates of the individual citizens of the Southern Confederate States, who were loyal to the South by President Lincoln as the chief executive of the United States and commander-in-chief of the Army; the success of the Federal forces and the downfall of the Confederacy having been assured by the surrender of Gen. Lee at Appomattox, on the 9th day of April, 1865, only five days before the final decision to take the life of President Lincoln. And I pause here to pay a tribute to the memory of Mrs. Surratt, for while she was hanged for her supposed connection with the conspiracy against the life of President Lincoln, she was innocent, and knew nothing whatever of the plot against the person to kidnap, or the final purpose to kill the President.

"It is true that I visited the home of Mrs. Surratt
in Washington; it is true I stopped at the Surratt
tavern, in Surrattville, not, however, because it was
the property of Mrs. Surratt, or that Mrs. Surratt
had anything to do with my being at the tavern, but
because it was the best, and I believe, the only place
for the traveling public to stop. in the village of
Surrattville. It is true that I was at the Surratt
home in Washington, but my mission there was to
see for the first time, by letter of introduction,
given me by a mutual friend, John H. Surratt, a son
of Mrs. Surratt, who was at the time in the secret
service of the Southern Confederacy as a spy, plying
in his service between Richmond, Virginia, Washington, D. C., New York City and Montreal, Canada, as
well as other points, as I was then informed. And it
was from John H. Surratt I desired to get information respecting what was then called the underground route, because of its hidden and isolated
way, over which Surratt traveled through the Federal lines en route from Richmond, Virginia, to
Washington, D. C., with the purpose of perfecting my
plans for the kidnaping of President Lincoln. This
occurred covering a time I should say from the
spring to the late summer of 1864. Prior to this
time I did not personally know, in fact, not even by
sight, John H. Surratt, and was informed that my

only chance to see him was to meet with him when he passed through Washington, D. C., when he would stop at his mother's home, at which place Mrs. Surratt was then keeping a boarding and lodging house. And this is the only purpose I had in going to Mrs. Surratt's home. Mrs. Surratt was at this time old enough to have been my mother, and I had only that casual acquaintance which my mission to the Surratt home had given me, and had only met her at intervals, and then for but a few moments at a time, covering the period and coupled with the crcumstances which I have mentioned as happening in 1864. And as a matter of fact at the final meeting with John H. Surratt our interview was of such a nature that he had no further knowledge of or connection with any conspiracy to kidnap, or later in the spring of 1865, to take the life of the President. This I say in justice to John H. Surratt, to the end also that Mrs. Surratt may live in the memory of the civilized people of the world as an innocent woman and without knowledge, guilty or otherwise, of the crime for which she was executed and whose blood stains the ermine of the judges of the military court condemning her to die. And could I do or say more in vindication of her name it would be gratifying, and would I had possession of Gabriel's horn and his mythical powers I would blow

38

one blast to wake the sleeping dead that this innocent woman might walk from the portals of the
house of death.''

To say that my breath was taken away almost by
this narrative is but a faint expression of my feelings, while St. Helen was perfectly calm with that
restful look which gives expression to a feeling of
relief.

CHAPTER VI.

THE ASSASSINATION

After a period of silence St. Helen began, with renewed interest and energy, telling me of the plot to kill President Lincoln, saying:

"On the morning of the day I killed the President the taking of the life of Mr. Lincoln had never entered my mind. My purpose had been, as I have stated, to kidnap President Lincoln for the purpose I have mentioned, and, in fact, one or more efforts to do so had fallen through, and we intended that the last effort should not fail. Preparatory to this end David E. Herold and I left Washington, D. C., by the way of Surrattville and along the underground route I have before described, for the purpose of perfecting plans for the kidnaping of the President. And after having passed over this line on horseback from Washington to near Richmond, Virginia, we returned, after making the necessary preparations for crossing the Potomac and Rappahanrock rivers, over the same route, stopping the night of the 13th day of April, 1865, at the old Surratt tavern, at Surrattville, located about twelve miles to the southeast of Washington City. On the morning of the 14th day of April, 1865, we came into Washington and were stopped at the block house of the Federal troops, at the bridge crossing the East Potomac river, by the Federal troops, on guard at this point. It appeared that some recent reports had been circulated that the life or safety of President Lincoln was impending, and that an attempt had or would be made from some source to assassinate the President, while at this time any such purpose was unknown to me, and because of these reports we were informed by the guard that no one could pass in or out of Washington City without giving a full account of himself, because of the threats against the life of the President. Herold and I hesitated to give our names for awhile, and were arrested and detained at this block house from about 11 o'clock in the morning until in the afternoon about 2 o'clock, when for the first time we heard definitely of Lee's surrender at Appomattox. We then realized that this was a death blow to the Southern Confederate States, when we made satisfactory explanation and were permitted to enter the city and went straight to the Kirkwood Hotel, the place of rendezvous of the conspirators against Mr. Lincoln, and where Andrew Johnson boarded. All the conspirators against President Lincoln met here with Andrew Johnson conversant of the purpose to kidnap the President. On arriving at the hotel, about 3 o'clock, I called on Vice-President

Johnson, when we talked over the situation and the changed conditions because of the surrender of Gen. Lee, and the Confederate forces at Appomattox, which had made the purpose of the kidnaping of President Lincoln and his delivery to the Confederate government at Richmond, to be held as a hostage of war, impossible, as the Confederate government had abandoned Richmond and the war between the States was considered practically over, which left, to my mind, nothing that we could do but accept defeat and leave the South, whom we had made our best efforts to serve, to her own fate, bitter and disappointing as it was. When Vice-President Johnson turned to me and said, in an excited voice and apparent anger:

" 'Will you falter at this supreme moment?'

"I could not understand his meaning, and stood silent, when with pale face, fixed eyes and quivering lips, Mr. Johnson asked of me:

" 'Are you too faint-hearted to kill him?'

"As God is my judge, this was the first suggestion of the dastardly deed of the taking of the life of President Lincoln, and came as a shock to me. While for the moment I waited and then said:

" 'To kill the President is certain death to me,' and I explained to Vice-President Johnson that I had just been arrested by the guard as I was com-

ANDREW JOHNSON.
Vice-President of the United States, and the Home Where
He Was Born, Near Raleigh, N. C.

JEFFERSON DAVIS.
President of the Confederate States of America During the
Late Civil War.

ing into the city over the East Potomac bridge that morning, and that it would be absolutely impossible for me to escape through the military line, should I do as he suggested, as this line of protection completely surrounded the city. Replying to this Mr. Johnson said:

" 'Gen. and Mrs. U. S. Grant are in the city, the guests of President Lincoln and family, and from the evening papers I have learned that President Lincoln and wife will entertain Gen. and Mrs. Grant at a box party to be given in their honor by the President and Mrs. Lincoln at Ford's Theater this evening.'

"At my suggestion Vice-President Johnson assured me that he would so arrange and see to it himself, that Gen. and Mrs. Grant would not attend the theater that evening with the President and his family, and would also arrange for my certain escape. I replied:

" 'Under these conditions and assurances I will dare strike the blow for the helpless, vanquished Southland, whose people I love.'

"Mr. Johnson left the room and after a little more than an hour returned, saying that it had been arranged as he had promised, and that Gen. Grant had been, or would be suddenly called from the city, and that, therefore, he and his wife could not attend

43

the theater that evening with the President and Mrs. Lincoln, as had been prearranged, and that such persons as would attend and occupy the box at the theater with the President and wife would not interfere with me in my purpose and effort to kill the President, and this he thought an opportune time, and that I would be permitted to escape by the route over which I had entered the city during the forenoon of that day. That is, that I was to go out over the East Potomac river bridge, that the guards would be called in from this point by order of Gen. C. C. Augur that afternoon or evening, but if there should be guards on the bridge, I was to use the password 'T. B.' or 'T. B. Road,' by explanation, if need be, which would be understood by the guards, and I would be permitted to pass and protected by himself (Mr. Johnson) absolutely in my escape, and that on the death of President Lincoln, he (Vice-President Johnson) would become president of the United States, and that in this official capacity I could depend on him for protection and absolute pardon, if need be, for the crime of killing President Lincoln, which he had suggested to me and I had agreed to perform.

"Fired by the thoughts of patriotism, and hoping to serve the Southern cause, hopeless as it then was, as no other man could then do, I regarded it as an opportunity for an heroic act for my country and not the exercise of a grudge or any feeling of malice toward the President, for I had none against him as an individual, but rather to slay the President that Andrew Johnson, a Southern man, a resident of the State of Tennessee, should be made President of the United States, to serve the interests of the South. And upon the further promise made me by Mr. Johnson that he as President of the United States, would protect the people of the South from personal oppression and the confiscation of their remaining landed estates, relying upon these promises, and believing that by the killing of President Lincoln I could practically bring victory to the Southern people out of defeat for the South. Moved by this purpose and actuated by no other motives, assured by Mr. Johnson of my personal safety, I began the preparation for the bloody deed by going to Ford's Theater, and among other things, arranging the door leading into the box to be occupied by Mr. Lincoln, which had already been decorated for the occasion, so that I could raise the fastenings, enter the box and close the door behind me so that it could not be opened from the outside and returned to the Kirkwood hotel. I then loaded afresh my derringer pistol so that she would not fail me of fire, and met Vice-President Johnson for the last time and informed him of my readiness to carry out the promise I had made him. About 8:30 that evening we left his room, walked to the bar in the hotel and drank strong brandy in a silent toast to the success of the bloody deed. We walked from the bar-room to the street together, when I offered my hand as the last token of good-bye and loyalty to our purpose, and I shall not forget to my dying day the clasp of his cold, clammy hand when he said:

" 'Make as sure of your aim as I have done in arranging for your escape. For in your complete success lies our only hope.'

"I replied, 'I will shoot him in the brain.'

" 'Then practically, from this time I am President of the United States,' replied Vice-President Johnson, and he added, 'good-bye.'

"I returned to the theater. I saw the President and party later take their seats in the box. I moved my position to a convenient space, and at the time when the way was clear and the play was well before the footlights I entered the President's box, closed the door behind me and instantly placed my pistol so near it almost touched his head and fired the shot which killed President Lincoln and made Andrew Johnson President of the United States and myself an outcast, a wanderer, and gave me the name of an assassin. As I fired the same instant I leaped from

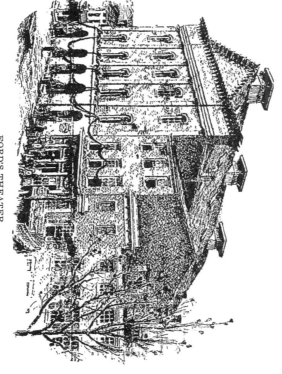

FORD'S THEATER.
The Scene of the Tragedy of the Assassination of President Lincoln.

Booth Fleeing from Ford's Theatre After the Assassination.

the box to the stage, my right spur entangled in something in the drapery on the box, which caused me to miss my aim or location on the stage and threw my shin bone against the edge of the stage, which fractured my right shin bone about six or eight inches above the ankle. (At this point St. Helen, exposing his shin, called attention to what seemed to be a niched or uneven surface on the shin bone. This I did not notice closely, but casually it appeared to have been a wound or fracture.)

"From the stage I reached my horse in safety, which by arrangement was being held by David E. Herold, back of the theater and close to the door of the back entrance. With Herold's assistance I mounted my horse and rode away with full speed without hindrance, and reached the bridge at the East Potomac river, crossing the same with my horse at full pace. When I came to the gate across the east end of the bridge there stood a Federal guard, who asked me a question easy to answer:

" 'Where are you going?'

"I replied, using the simple letters 'T. B.' as I had been instructed, and the guard then asked:

" 'Where?'

"I then replied, 'T. B. Road,' as I had been instructed by Mr. Johnson, and without further question the guard called for assistance to help raise the gate quickly, when I at once again urged my horse to full speed and went on to Surrattville, where I waited for Herold to overtake me, as prearranged, whom I expected to follow closely behind. After waiting a few minutes Herold came up and we rode the remainder of the night until about 4 o'clock on the morning of the 15th of April, 1865, when we reached the home of Dr. Samuel Mudd, where Dr. Mudd, by cutting a slit in it, removed my riding boot from the injured right foot and leg and proceeded to dress it by bandaging it with strips of cloth and pieces of cigar boxes, and the riding boot was left at the home of Dr. Mudd, where we remained during the rest of the day, and at nightfall proceeded on our journey, my bootless right foot being covered only by the sock and the leg as bandaged and splinted by Dr. Mudd.

"From the home of Dr. Mudd I went to the home of a Southern sympathizer by the name of Cox, which we reached between 4 and 5 o'clock on the morning of the 16th day of April, 1865. Mr. Cox refused to admit us into his house, the news of the death of President Lincoln having preceded us, and he feared for this reason to take Herold and me in. But he called his overseer, or manager about the place, and instructed him to hide us in a pine thicket on or near the banks of the Potomac river, just back of and near his plantation. This man, the overseer, was of medium size, approximately my weight, but not quite so tall, I should say, swarthy complexioned, black hair and eyes, with a short growth of whiskers over his face. I called him by that familiar cognomen known to the Confederate soldiers, 'Johnny.' I have the impression, whether correct or not I cannot say, from having heard his name called by a Mr. Jones, a relative of Mr. Cox, that it was Ruddy or Roby, but heard this only a few times. Of course, this may have been a given name, nickname or sirname, I don't know how this was; I was not specially interested in knowing his name and was with him but a short while, having negotiated with him to put us across the country and into the care and protection of the Confederate soldiers.

"Ruddy told me (if this be his name) that some of Col. Mosby's command of Confederate troops was then encamped not far south of the Rappahannock river at or near Bowling Green, Virginia, and agreed to convey and deliver us to these Confederate troops for a price, as I now best remember, about three hundred dollars. Ruddy, as we will call him, left us in our hiding place until he could go to Bowling Green, some thirty-five miles or more distant, with a view of arranging with some of these soldiers to meet us at a fixed time and place—proposedly on the Rappahannock river, which was then about the dividing line between the contending Federal and Confederate armies.

"Ruddy left and did not return for several days, from say the 16th or 17th to the 21st of April, 1865. Herold and I were cared for during his absence by Mr. Jones, the relative, I think, half brother of Mr. Cox. On Ruddy's return he reported that the desired arrangements had been made with Capt. Jett and others of Mosby's command, then stationed at Bowling Green, Virginia, south of the Rappahannock river, to meet us at the ferry on the Rappahannock river at Ports Conway and Royal, as early as 2 o'clock P. M. of April 22, 1865. So we immediately started for this point on the night of the 21st of April, crossed the Potomac river, reaching the south side of the Potomac river we then had about eighteen miles to go from the Potomac to the Rappahannock river to the point agreed upon. This distance was through an open country, and we were liable to be come upon at any moment by the Federal troops; so to guard against this I arranged the plan of my flight, covering this distance from the Potomac to the Rappahannock to be the scene of an old negro moving. An old negro near the summer home of Dr. Stewart possessed of two impoverished horses and a dilapidated wagon was hired for the trip.

Straw was first placed in the bottom of the wagon bed. I got in on this straw and stretched out full length; then slats were placed over the first compartment of the bed, giving me a space of about eighteen inches deep, which required me to remain lying on the straw during the entire trip. On the first compartment of the wagon bed was placed the second portion of the wagon body, commonly called sideboards, then was piled on this old chairs, beds, mattresses, quilts and such other paraphernalia as is ordinarily kept in a negro's home. A number of chickens were caught and put in a split basket, which was then made fast to the hind gate of the wagon, with old quilts, blankets, etc., thrown over the back end of the wagon, exposing the basket of chickens, and the wagon or team was driven by the old negro, the owner of the same, and contents, except myself. And now having this arrangement perfect in all details, we at once, about 6 o'clock A.M., left on our perilous trip from the Potomac to the Rappahannock river with Ports Conway and Royal as our destination, covering the distance of about eighteen or twenty miles without incident or accident on our march; Herold and Ruddy following along in the wake of the wagon, some distance behind, they told me, so as not to detract from the scene of the plot which was to be taken as one of an old negro moving.

"In my concealment, of course, I had to be very quiet. I could not talk to old Lewis, the old negro driver, and made myself as comfortable as I could be in my cramped position. In my side coat pocket I had a number of letters, together with my diary, and I think there was a picture of my sister, Mrs. Clark, all of which must have worked out of my pocket en route or came out as I was hurriedly taken from the wagon. Just as we drew up at the ferry old Lewis called out:

" 'Dar's dem soldiers now.'

"And at the same moment some one began tearing away the things from the back gate of the wagon, who proved to be Herold and Ruddy, much to my relief, as they had begun unceremoniously to remove the back gate of the wagon, which necessarily excited me very much, as the driver did not say Confederate soldiers, and the 'soldiers' referred to flashed through my brain as being Federal soldiers. But before I can tell you the back of the wagon was taken away, I was pulled out by the heels by Harold and Ruddy, and at once hustled into the ferry boat and over the river, where our Confederate friends were waiting for us. They, in fact, being the 'soldiers' referred to by Lewis, the driver.

"In the hurry, as well as the method of taking me from the wagon, I think the letters, diary and picture of my sister, were lost from my pocket, as I was dragged out. About this I can't say, but I do know that after I had crossed the river and was feeling in my pocket to get the check, which I had on a Canadian bank, and with which I paid this man Ruddy for his services he had rendered us, for an amount, as I now remember it, of about sixty pounds, I discovered I had lost these papers. I asked Ruddy to go back over the river and get them out of the wagon, if they were there, and bring them to me at the Garrett home, where the soldiers had arranged to take me until Herold and Ruddy should go to Bowling Green, Virginia, that afternoon, it being then about 2 o'clock.

"This man Ruddy stepped into an old batteau boat to go over to the wagon and get these papers after I handed him his check. We being too exposed to wait for his return, I hurriedly rode away with the two gentlemen to whom I had been introduced as Lieuts. Ruggles and Bainbridge, to the Garrett home, mounted on a horse belonging to the man to whom I had been introduced as Capt. Jett. These gentlemen, as I understood it, were connected with Mosby's command of Confederate soldiers. But before separating at this ferry it had been understood between Herold, Ruddy and myself that they would go to Bowling Green, Virginia, that afternoon, in company with Capt. Jett, on foot, by a near way, for the purpose of getting me a shoe for my lame foot and such other things as Herold and I needed and that could not be obtained at Ports Conway and Royal, and they were to return and meet me the next day at the Garrett home, where Ruddy would deliver to me the papers mentioned, if recovered.

"The Garrett home, I should say, is about three miles north of the public road crossing the Rappahannock river at Ports Conway and Royal and leading in a southerly direction to Bowling Green, Virginia. From the ferry we went out the Bowling Green road a short distance westerly; we then turned and rode north on a country or bridle road for a distance of about three miles and a half, when we reached the Garrett home, where Lieuts. Bainbridge and Ruggles left me, but were to keep watch in the distance over me until Ruddy and Herold returned, which they were expected to do the following day, it being some twelve or fifteen miles walk for them. They were to remain there (at Bowling Green) over night of the day they left me and return the following day.

"About one or two o'clock in the afternoon of April the 23d, 1865, the second day of my stay at the Garrett home, I was out in the front yard, lounging on the meadow, when Lieuts. Bainbridge and

Ruggles came up hurriedly and notified me that a squad of Yankee troops had crossed the Rappahannock river in hot pursuit of me, and advised me to leave at once and go back into the woods north of the Garrett house, in a wooded ravine, which they pointed out, giving me a signal whistle by which I would know them, and hurriedly rode off, saying that they would return for me in about an hour at the place designated, and bring with them a horse for my escape.

"I left immediately, without letting anyone know that I had gone or the direction I had taken. I reached the woods at about the place which had been pointed out to me, as nearly as one could traveling in a strange wooded section with the impediment of a lame leg. At about the time fixed I was delighted to hear the signal, and answered, to the best of my recollection, about three or four o'clock P. M. My friends came up with an extra horse, which I mounted, and we rode away in a westerly direction, riding the remainder of the afternoon and the following night until about twelve o'clock, when we camped together in the woods, or rather dismounted to rest ourselves and horses until daylight. We talked over the situation, they giving me directions by which I should travel. When we at last separated in a country road, they said about twenty or twenty-five miles to the west of the Garrett home or Ports Royal and Conway; I, of course, thanked them and offered them pay for the services they had rendered me and the price of the horse they had turned over to me, all of which they refused to accept, and bade me goodbye, with the warning that I should keep my course well to the westward for that day's ride, and then, after this day's ride, continue my journey to the southwest.

"As advised by them, I rode on westerly through all the country roads as I came to them leading in that direction until about ten o'clock A.M. of the second day out from the Garrett home, when, owing to the fatigue of myself and horse, and suffering from my wounded leg, I found it necessary to rest and stopped at a small farm house on the country road, where there seemed to live only three elderly ladies, who, at my request, took me in as a wounded Confederate soldier, fed my horse and gave me breakfast, and as I now best remember, I compensated them, paying them one dollar in small silver coin.

"After a few hours' rest for myself and horse, I pushed on toward the west the remainder of the day and the forepart of the night, as best I could, but early in the night I rode into the thick brush located in a small creek bottom some distance from

THE SUMMER HOME OF DR. STEWART.
Near Where Was Obtained the Old Negro and His Wagon to
Haul Booth to the Rappahannock River.

Booth, Disguised as a Confederate Soldier in His Flight,
Applies for Shelter and Hospitality for His Tired Horse
and Himself.

the road and remained there all night. The next morning I obtained breakfast for myself and feed for my horse from an elderly gentleman and lady at a little country home at an early hour without further incident and interest, save and except the enjoyment of the meal, when I turned my course to the southwest, as I had been directed, and followed this direction day after day, impersonating the character of a Confederate soldier. Continuing on down through West Virginia, I crossed the Big Sandy river at Warfield, in Eastern Kentucky, and after traveling from Warfield for about two days, and covering a distance of fifty or sixey miles in a southwesterly direction from Warfield, I, as well as my horse, was about worn out, and I was therefore compelled to rest for about a week, claiming to be a wounded Confederate soldier. The parties with whom I stopped was a widow lady and her young son, whose name I can not now remember. But after receiving their kind attentions and needed rest, I resumed my journey with the purpose of traveling to the south until I could reach the Mississippi river at a safe point for crossing it, and find my way into the Indian Territory as the best possible hiding place, in my opinion.

"I finally reached without incident worthy of mention the Mississippi river and crossed the same at what was called Catfish Point, in the State of Mississippi. This point is a short distance south of where the Arkansas river empties into the Mississippi river. I followed the south and west bank of the Arkansas river until I reached the Indian Territory, where I remained at different places, hiding among the Indians for about eighteen months, when I left the Indian Territory and went to Nebraska and was at Nebraska City employed by a white man to drive a team connected with a wagon train going from Nebraska City, Nebraska, to Salt Lake City, Utah. This man was hauling provisions for the United States government to the Federal troops encamped at Salt Lake City. But I left this wagon train while en route, just before we got to Salt Lake City, and proceeded to San Francisco, California, to meet my mother and my brother, Junius Brutus Booth. After meeting my mother and brother and remaining a while there, I left and went into Mexico. From there I went up through Texas, finally stopping at Glenrose Mills and Grandberry, Texas, where we are now.

"Of course, I could add many matters of interest to what I have said to you, but I have told you quite sufficient for the present," saying which he gave me a look of inquiry as much as to say, "Well, what do you thing of me now?"

THE ASSASSINATION.

I broke my long, intense and interested silence by saying, as I rose from my seat and looked at my watch:

"It is now about our lunch hour; suppose we return to town," to which St. Helen assented.

CHAPTER VII.

THE MAN KILLED AT THE GARRETT HOME

As we were returning to town I continued the subject of our conversation by saying to St. Helen that I had little knowledge of the history of the matters about which he had spoken so in detail, but as of general information knew that John Wilkes Booth had assassinated President Lincoln, though had no accurate knowledge of the facts as detailed by him of the President's assassination, such as would enable me to reach the conclusion, as to the correctness or incorrectness of his statement, for I having been a small boy at the close of the Civil War had not had the opportunity to know much of the history of the war, and less of the facts touching the tragic death of President Lincoln, and therefore was left alone to judge of the truth of what he said by the impressions and convictions that his mere relation of it created on my mind. The truth being that I did not believe his story and sought the first opportunity to close an interview as abhorrent as it was disbelievable by me. And out of charity I had begun to regard St. Helen as an insane man, bordering in fact upon violent madness, but I said to him:

"I have learned to know and like you as John St. Helen, but I would not know how to regard you and associate with you as John Wilkes Booth, the assassin, and to be kind and generous to you as my friend, I must say I do not believe your story. First because, I like St. Helen, and in the second place is it not true that John Wilkes Booth was killed soon after the assassination of President Lincoln, such as has been the general information heretofore practically unquestioned? No, St. Helen, not against my will and in face of these facts can I believe you the assassin and criminal you claim to be. And giving you the benefit of the doubt of your sanity I must decline to accept your story as true. It is possible you may have known Booth and the secrets of his crime and escape, and it is possible that from your brooding over this subject your mind has become shaken and you imagine yourself Booth. To me you are my friend John St. Helen— not the wicked and arch-criminal, the assassin, John Wilkes Booth. It would take even more than your sane statement to make me believe that you are any other than John St. Helen. I can't believe that one of your humane instincts, possessed, as I think I know you to be, of all the attributes of gentle breeding and

61

culture, with the highest order of intellect and refinement blended with beautiful sentiment, and possessed of a soul unalloyed with crime, can be John Wilkes Booth. Could a man seemingly possessed of such attributes, protected by a strong manhood, without physical or mental fear, without an apparent taint of the composition of cowardice, play the part of an assassin? Booth may have been possessed of all the qualities that it takes to make up the assassin, but St. Helen? In my opinion, no, if I mistake not your character. You would have met the man you sought to slay to the forefront and bid him with equal chance defend the life you would take.

"Then, too, did not the government of the United States announce to the American people, and as for that matter, to the civilized world, that Booth was killed and the death of President Lincoln avenged? Then do you say it is a fact that Booth was not killed at the Garrett barn in Virginia? It is a physical fact that some man was killed at the Garrett home. If not Booth who was this man?"

St. Helen replied by saying, "As you have heard that a man was killed at the Garrett barn, and without positive or direct proof as to who this man was, yet from the circumstances I would say that it was Ruddy, the man with whom I had negotiated for my personal deliverance, together with that of my accomplice, David E. Herold, to the Confederate soldiers. You will remember I paid this man with a check made payable to my order by a Canadian bank, and if he did, as I requested, which he promised to do and left me to do, he got my letters, pictures, etcetera, out of the wagon, as I have explained to you, as he was to bring them to me at the Garrett home on the day or night following the day that I left the Garrett home, as I have also explained to you. I take it, without personal knowledge of the facts, that Ruddy and Herold came to the Garrett home, as prearranged and promised when we separated at the ferry on the Rappahannock river, so that the Federal troops, by some means, traced me to the Garrett home, where they found Herold and Ruddy, killing Ruddy and capturing Herold. They found on the body of Ruddy the check for sixty pounds, together with my letters, and I think a picture, and by reason of finding these belongings of mine on the body of Ruddy, I presume they identified it as the body of myself. But this misleading incident, for I take it to be true that these documents unexplained found upon the body of anyone, and surely by those who did not know me, would reasonably and rightfully justify the conclusion that they had the body of John Wilkes Booth, but they were in fact mistaken. And I do not for one moment doubt the sincerity of the individual members of the government or officers and men who captured Herold and killed, as I suppose, Ruddy, in believing that they had killed me, and it was certainly a reasonable and justifiable mistake if they had no other means of identifying me than the check and documents found on the man or body of the man whom we have called Ruddy. But in this connection I desire to say, so that my conscience shall be clear and confession complete, that I have no cause to complain of the treatment that I have received at the hands of the Federal soldiers or officers in pursuit of me before and after the killing of President Lincoln, for they were more than once in plain and broad view of me. It is a little remarkable, don't you think, that it was possible for me to remain within the Federal lines for seven or more entire days and nights, within forty miles of Washington City, in a country entirely open and within the territory completely occupied by the Federal troops, while I waited for Ruddy to go within the Confederate lines and arrange to have Confederate soldiers meet us at the Rappahannock river, as the safest and most certain means of my escape?"

"Then, it is your contention, St. Helen, that the circumstances of finding your letters, etc., on Ruddy's body was all the proof they had?"

THE MAN KILLED AT THE GARRETT HOME.

"Certainly, they could have only had circumstantial proof—not having killed me. They could only reach the conclusion from the incident mentioned, and I am before you now as a physical monument to .the fact that I was not killed."

"Yes, but I, in my opinion, as well as a large majority of the American people, believe that the government has in its possession absolute and positive proof of the killing and death of Booth. However this may be, I shall continue to know and associate with you only as John St. Helen, until I shall have more satisfactory proof of your identity," when so saying St. Helen and I separated and went our different ways to a late luncheon. While I as a fact had little or no confidence in the story told me by St. Helen and did not believe St. Helen to be Booth, still his manner, directness and detail of his statement left its impress on me and gave a justifiable cause for serious reflection.

The former pleasant relation between St. Helen and myself could not be continued with him as Booth, for we forget to recognize merit and friendship in one's character where there is much to be otherwise condemned. In fact we find our friendship paling to contempt and our admiration to scorn. The criminal becomes common place and unattractive, because he is unworthy, regardless of his physical attractiveness

65

or mental attainments. We recognize in him the villain. What we may call St. Helen's confession tended to clear up the mystery he had thrown around himself when he sought to avoid his appearance before the Federal court at Tyler, by saying his true name was not St. Helen, and I now think of his confession in the light of his hard fight and the payment of money to avoid being taken within the settled and civilized sections of the state of Texas, lest he should be identified to be another than John St. Helen. This was a suspicious circumstance, at least, that in fact St. Helen was Booth, or some other man than St. Helen, for as a fact if he was Booth it was possible and highly probable that he would have been identified by some of the court officials, especially by the United States District Attorney, Col. Jack Evans, who it is more than probable had seen John Wilkes Booth on the stage. Knowing the District Attorney as I did, as also from information of his frequent trips to Washington and Eastern cities during the days of Booth's triumphs before the footlights would show a well founded reason why St. Helen should not have taken the risk incident to a trip to Tyler, if in fact he was Booth. Then I would think he could have been equally as well John St. Helen, John Smith or John Brown, or any other man, who had committed some crime other than that of the assassination of President Lincoln, for the commission of which he would have been equally as anxious to avoid detection under any other name or for any other crime, if such crime had any connection with the violation of the Federal law. In other words, he could as well have been a mail robber as the assassin of a President. So, that I could place but little importance in these statements and circumstances as a proof that St. Helen was in fact John Wilkes Booth, but rather thought of his confession as an evidence of an identity not yet spoken of. So that the true identity of this mysterious St. Helen became more mystifying. Then I would think of what St. Helen had said when he thought he was making his dying declaration that he was John Wilkes Booth. And if this was not true why need he in the presence of impending death, as he thought, make the confession that he was Booth? Then, too, I would think this confession was without significance, as St. Helen seemed prompted by no purpose after he had been saved from the Federal court and from death, except to prove to me the fact of his true identity, for what interest could it have been to me or what could it avail Booth, his purpose having been accomplished? So reasoning from the standpoint of cause or motives the conclusions reached were first, that St. Helen was not Booth, because he disclosed his secret without an apparent necessity, or from a business point of view, and not likely from a matter of sentiment. Then I would think, is the man demented? And is he living without purpose or reason? Or is he conscience stricken and telling the truth for the relief that its confession brings to him? And thus can reason answer?

Resting in this state of mind I waited an opportune time when St. Helen and myself were retired, effectually hidden from intrusion, and expressed to him my apprehension of his perfect sanity as well as of his true identity, and asked him to more fully explain why he had made this confession to me at a time when he supposed he was in his last illness that he was John Wilkes Booth. And that if as a matter of fact he was John Wilkes Booth, why he wanted me to know it. St. Helen, without hesitation but with slow and deliberate expression in substance said:

"I have spoken to you in good faith and in very truth, having in no way deceived or in any manner misled you, and had thought in the statements I have made you I had clearly shown my purpose. But having failed in this I realize my fault, possibly produced by my long habit of secretiveness of purpose, that my conversations may more or less partake of the long hidden mystery of my life, and in themselves appear mystifying and contradictory in a measure to the

68

legal mind. But you will remember that I gave you these reasons some time ago—that it was first a duty I owe myself and family name that the world might know the motives for my crime. Then, too, I reflect, that my crime is possibly without palliation, certainly has no justifying excuse in the eyes of the world. That in fact the greater part of my purpose in the confession I first made you was to secure my release from an attendance on the Federal court. Other than this selfish motive you can not easily understand, and now in the light of what I have said to you I must confess that I, in fact, think that I was moved by a desire of finding a confidant to whom at a chance risk of my life I could speak fully of my identity and unburdened the story of my crime to you, for God and the criminal himself only know the punishment it is for one not to be able to take his trouble to a friend and unfold his mind to the ear which will listen with pity, if not approval, and at least share with him the knowledge of his crime. To you, free from crime, it will doubtless occur that this could at most be but little consolation, but don't forget that any consolation at all is better than none, and that the life of man at best is but a parasite on the life of others; his friends who give hope of the impossible to himself make life worth the living, and friendships kindled into faith become the beacon fires which illumine the hours of our darkness beyond the sunlights of today, and through the shadowed valley to the great beyond where God rules and Justice obtains throughout the time of all eternity.

"After all, be it so. Having made known to you my true identity and the cause of my crime, although I know that you by your actions condemn me in fact, I would think less of you if you did not, for I myself confess, and would the power I had to condemn that which you condemn, conscious that the Arbiter of our being is pitiless in accusation, ever present in persecution and tireless in punishment. Yes, I walk in the companionship of crime, sleep within the folds of sin and dream the dreams of the damned and awake to go forth by all men accused as well as self-condemned. Ah, aweary, aweary! Shall I say that I would that I were dead? Yes, that I could on the wings of the wind, by a starless and moonless night, be gone in flight to the land of perpetual silence, where I could forget and be forgotten, and whisper to my weary soul, 'Peace, be still.' But for me, except in death, there is no rest, for God in the dispensation of His justice ordains that the criminal shall suffer the pangs of his own crime. Why, then, should I hope? But hopeless I may turn when all nature is hushed and hear the voice of the supernatural saying:

THE MAN KILLED AT THE GARRETT HOME.

" 'Look, Repent and Confess.' When shines within the light of the star of Bethlehem I shall see extended to me the outstretched arms of the Sainted Mother Mary, I look, repent and confess, and the fires of hope shall rekindle at the urn of my being, with the fagots of incense burning in holy light giving off the perfume of frankincense and myrrh—a food for and a purification of the soul. And this alone can bring relief to my physical and spiritual being. And in my confession to you I appealed for the pity of man that I might live in common knowledge with some one man, the secret that I, John Wilkes Booth, did make my escape after the killing of President Lincoln, whose life to replace I would gladly give my own."

When I said to St. Helen, drop the curtain on the beautiful sentiments expressed and for awhile listen to me. The statements that you made with reference to Mrs. Surratt and her son John Surratt can readily be accepted as reasonable, but if you mean to say that Vice-President, Andrew Johnson, was the leading conspirator and had formed a plan to kidnap and finally suggested the assassination of President Lincoln, it is startling to a point of disbelief, an insult to American manhood! It traduces the character of a dead man, and is equalled only by the depravity and cowardice characterizing the act of the assassination of President Lincoln. No! I can not yet without more proof believe the statement that you make to be a fact. What reason, I pray, could Andrew Johnson have in being a party to the assassination of President Lincoln under the circumstances, or even under other circumstances than such as you have stated?''

St. Helen, replying in substance, said:

''I am not unmindful of what my statements imply and weigh the consequences as well as measure my words, when I say that in the light of after events, it was in fact Vice-President Johnson's only purpose in planning and causing the assassination of President Lincoln, to make himself President of the United States, but he then gave as his reason, among others, which I have before explained to you, that President Lincoln, by the act of the emancipation of the slaves of the South, had violated the constitutional rights of property of the Southern people and reasoned that if he would override the Constitution of the United States in this respect that Mr. Lincoln was a dangerous man to be President, for that he could with the same propriety and that he would in his (Mr. Johnson's) opinion continue his policy of the confiscation of the remaining properties of the people of the South. That he (Mr. Johnson) was a Southern man and a citizen resident of the South, and it was reasonable to expect, believe, and in fact know, that he would do more for the South under the then existing conditions than President Lincoln, who, Mr. Johnson contended, was the South's greatest enemy, saying that he (Mr. Johnson) was present at a cabinet meeting prior to September 22nd, 1864, by invitation of President Lincoln, when the question of the emancipation of slavery was to be discussed and that upon this occasion it was developed that five out of seven members of President Lincoln's cabinet, as follows, Wells, Smith, Seward, Blair and Bates, were opposed to the issuance and promulgation of the emancipation proclamation, and the argument made by those men in opposition was that such a proclamation by the chief executive, overriding the decision of the Supreme Court of the United States in the Dred Scott case, was an usurpation of the law and constitution of the United States. To this President Lincoln replied:

" 'The legal objections raised in opposition to the promulgation of the Emancipation Proclamation freeing the negro slaves of the United States is well founded and true, but I believe it would be a vital stroke against our sister states in rebellion, and believing this as I do, as Commander-in-Chief of the Army and as President of the United States, I shall issue this proclamation as a war measure, believing it to be my official duty. Believing, as I do, that the free-

dom of the negroes is humane and meritorious and a
blow to the enemy which it can not long withstand,
and from my understanding of my official dual capacity as President of the United States as its Civil
Officer and Commander-in-Chief of the Army from a
military standpoint, I violate no law or official trust
in doing what in my opinion is best and just in the
suppression of the present rebellion.'

" 'This act of President Lincoln,' continued Mr.
Johnson, 'Was earnest of his policy to be carried out
toward the subjugated South.'

"This reasoning at the time seemed unselfish and
logical, and I agreed with him that the supreme moment for the displacement of President Lincoln had
arrived. And if you will think for a moment of the
conditions as they obtained at that time, in Washington City, you will agree with me that it was impossible
for me, a mere citizen, a civilian without influence,
except through Vice-President Johnson, with either
the civil or military powers at Washington, I being in
no way connected with the Federal or Confederate
armies and following my vocation as an actor, at my
convenience and pleasure, that it was a physical impossibility for me to have arranged my escape through
the Federal lines, then completely surrounding Washington, through which I had to go and did pass after
the accomplishment of the death of President Lincoln,

for at this time, as it had been practically during the entire Civil War, Washington City was closely guarded by a cordon of soldiers thrown completely around it, making it impossible to pass in or out of the city without passing through this well-guarded line, and this only could be done by officially recognized permits, and even with these permits one could not pass into the city without giving a full account of himself.

"Now, do you think that I unaided could have arranged for my escape? Then, think, Gen. U. S. Grant and wife, as you know, were to attend the theatre with President and Mrs. Lincoln on that evening, and I could not have undertaken to go into the closed box so unequally matched as I would have been with both President Lincoln and Gen. Grant there. So, the absence of Gen. Grant was arranged. Could I do this? History records the fact that Gen. Grant was suddenly called from the City of Washington late in the afternon of the evening of the assassination of President Lincoln. You understand that Gen. and Mrs. Grant were the guests of the President and Mrs. Lincoln, receiving the congratulations of Mr. Lincoln as Commander-in-Chief of the Army, only five days after the surrender of Gen. Lee—accepting the hospitality of the President and Mrs. Lincoln, a compliment extended to Gen. Grant on account of his great achievement in the defeat of Robert E. Lee and his army before Richmond, at Appomatox, and this entertainment at Ford's theater was a part of the program for their entertainment, and was to mark the first public appearance together of President Lincoln and Gen. Grant as the greatest heroes of the Civil War connected with the Federal army. Whether Gen. Grant's absence was a mere incident I can not say. I only know that Vice-President Johnson informed me only a few hours before the killing of President Lincoln that Gen. Grant would not be in attendance with President Lincoln at the theatre. How he knew it, I do not know. But I do know that I would not have gone into the box and locked myself inside so unevenly matched as I would have been with Gen. Grant present, and had he been present President Lincoln would not have been killed by me on that evening. Knowing from the evening papers of the intended presence of Gen. Grant, one of my conditions for attempting the life of the President was that Gen. Grant should not be present, and it is a physical fact that he was not there. Take the further physical fact that I did kill the President, and that I did pass out of the lines, as directed by Mr. Johnson, without molestation at the same point where I had been arrested and detained on the morning of the same day I killed the President; that I approached the same guarded spot with my horse under whip and spur, at or about 10:30 o'clock at night, when upon giving the pass word T. B. or T. B. Road to the Federal soldiers then guarding the gate at the bridge, I was allowed to pass out. The guard at once called for the assistance of another guard standing close by, and the gate was hurriedly raised and without further question I rode through, put spur to my horse and was off again as fast as the animal could go.

"Likewise, Herold, my accomplice, was permitted to cross the bridge by the same guard, by the use of the same pass word, and came up with me at Surratt-ville. These physical facts stand as undeniable proof of my official aid and my escape! Taking these facts into consideration, who can say or doubt for one moment that I was assisted by one, or more, persons high in official circles, as well as in military life?"

"Then, St. Helen, do you mean to say that Gen. Grant was a party to or cognizant of the plot against the life of President Lincoln?"

"No, I do not. All I know is that I was informed by Vice-President Johnson that Gen. Grant was to be in the box with President Lincoln on that evening. I told him I could not undertake to carry out the plan against the life of the President, as I have stated, should Gen. Grant remain in the box, that is, should he attend the theatre and occupy the box with Mr. Lincoln. Mr. Johnson left me late that afternoon to arrange for my escape and on his return, before giving me instructions for my escape, he said that Gen. Grant would not be present. How he knew this I can not say. All I can say is to repeat what I have said. All the world knows that Gen. and Mrs. Grant were not in the box. From these existing physical facts, with no accusation by innuendo, or otherwise, you must draw your own conclusions. My own fixed opinion upon this subject, however, I am free to express to you—and I confess that I do not believe that Gen. Grant knew of any arrangements being made to kill President Lincoln. I believe rather that he had been decoyed off by some means, unsuspected by him, and certainly not known to me, as were also other instances apparently connected with the assassination of the President. For instance, I knew nothing of any plan to take the life of Secretary Seward on the night of the assassination of President Lincoln, or at any other time, showing that it would appear to have been a conspiracy against both the President and certain members of the Cabinet.''

''While your story may be true, St. Helen, and is apparently sustained by the facts which you state, considering your statements to be facts, and I have no information for a successful denial, if all you say is true, it in no way identifies you as John Wilkes Booth. Your story could be as well told by any one else of your genius for some purpose hidden from me, so I must continue to know you as John St. Helen.''

St. Helen replied, ''Then allow me to say that your long and persistent reasoning that I am not John Wilkes Booth almost persuades me that I am in fact John St. Helen. Indeed, I am quite willing that you shall believe I am not John Wilkes Booth. However, I realize that you have one proof of my identity— my tintype picture. I ask that you will keep that picture, which may be the means of my complete identification to you some day, when you will better understand that my confidence in you has been prompted by selfish motives to a certain degree. While your continued mistrust and disbelief is comforting to me, in that I reflect that you, after all that I have told you, for the reasons that you have given, are not willing to believe me the criminal that I am; or, if this disbelief arises from your thinking me incapable of the crime to which I plead guilty, it is surely gratifying. But, if on the other hand, your mistrust arises from your opinion that I am unworthy of belief under any and all circumstances, my purposes are thwarted and my efforts of no avail. But remember always that I am grateful to you for what you have done for me, and the burden you share with me, unwittingly, whether it be with St. Helen or with Booth, and in the future as in the past, with your permission, we will be friends. Think of me as you will, my true name and identity you have. My correct personality you know, and whether we long associate together or soon separate, remember you are the one man—the only living man with whom I leave the true story of the tragedy which ended the life of President Lincoln."

Closing with this statement, St. Helen left me in an uncertain frame of mind. The future standing as a barrier against coming events I was not prepared at that time to admit that St. Helen was Booth. I was unwilling to assume the responsibility of believing that St. Helen was Booth. Aside from my better judgment was my strong faith in the accuracy of the claims of my government that John Wilkes Booth, the assassin, had been killed, and I did not care to acquire the unpleasant notoriety and criticism of making the announcement that John Wilkes Booth in fact lived, unless the proof of such a fact was established irrefutably. So, I determined to drop the subject for all time to come—treating it as a myth unfounded in fact—a story that existed only in the mind of St. Helen, a comparatively demented man, a crank, who gloried in deceiving me to the idea. I preferred to accept the story of the event referred to as it is told by the government—the accepted facts of history rather than those of this man of mystery. And in our after association, lasting about ten months, we made no further reference to the subject, which was avoided by mutual consent.

Aside from this unpleasant side of St. Helen's character he was modest, unobtrusive and congenial, ever pleasant in association with me. He was a social favorite with all with whom he came in contact, yet, he was rather the social autocrat than the social democrat. Except for a select few he held all men to the strictest social etiquette, repelling all undue familiarity, refusing all overtures of social equality with even those of the better middle classes of men, but it was done in such a gentle and respectful way that no affront was taken—if such it could be called, it was more pleasant than otherwise, leaving the impression that he, St. Helen, would be delighted to be on the most intimate terms with the other, but, as there is nothing in common between us more than a respectful speaking relation, it is an impossibility. And thus he made friends while he drew the social lines and pressed home a consciousness of his own superiority as an entertainer.

The hours of our social life were pleasantly spent, not by riotous living but by amusing games of cards, recitations and readings by St. Helen, which were always a great treat, and which he himself seemed to enjoy, as did his friends.

St. Helen often admitted that in his younger days he sometimes drank to excess of strong whiskeys, wines, etc., as also decoctions of brandy and cordials, but during our associations I never knew of his taking strong drink of any character, nor did he use tobacco in any form, and in the absence of these habits and tastes we were entirely congenial, as I myself had never cultivated appetites of this character. We were also lovers of literature of the same class, as well as music and the fine arts, and matters pertaining to the stage. We enjoyed the gossip of the stage, and the people of the stage came in for a large share of our attention, especially St. Helen's, who talked much of what he called the old and the new school of acting, with which I became conversant, which greatly pleased St. Helen, who frequently made reference to me as his trained associate, while he would explain that men became congenial by constant association linked together by the common mother, kindred thoughts, the offspring of blended characters.

CHAPTER VIII.

THE SEPARATION

St. Helen had grown tired of his class of business. In fact, he paid little attention to it, letting it drift with the tide of business affairs in the little town of Grandberry. Now his mind turned to thoughts of mining and the acquisition of wealth by the development of mining properties in Colorado. I was looking to other fields for my efforts and decided to leave Texas.

When the final hour of our separation came I returned to the States, as we Westerners termed the older States in the Union, and St. Helen left for Leadville, Colorado, in the spring of 1878, from which point I lost trace of him until some time in the year 1898. In the meantime I had located in the city of Memphis, Tennessee, and St. Helen and I were far apart—lost to each other and comparatively forgotten for a period of twenty years.

During this interval of time, my location being more convenient to books and the acquiring of information, I investigated the subject of the assassination of President Lincoln and its attendant circumstances in view of the statements made by St. Helen. He had connected Andrew Johnson with the plot to kidnap and assassinate President Lincoln and investigation became interesting to learn, if possible, the relations, personal and otherwise, existing between President Lincoln and Vice-President Andrew Johnson.

In this search I find that the oath of office as President of the United States was administered to Andrew Johnson by Chief Justice Chase in the lodgings of Andrew Johnson, at the Kirkwood Hotel, Washington, D. C., and that besides members of the Cabinet a number of United States Senators were called in to witness the ceremony. At this hour but few of the citizens of Washington knew that President Lincoln was dead. The inauguration occurred at 10 o'clock on the morning of April 15, 1865, President Lincoln having died at twenty-two minutes past 7 o'clock on the same morning.

At his informal inauguration President Johnson made a speech remarkable in that he made no mention of President Lincoln. I give this speech in part with the comments thereon by those present, who say:

"The effect produced upon the public by this speech, which might be regarded as an inaugural address, was not happy. Besides its evasive character respecting public policies, which every observant man noted, with apprehension, an unpleasant impression was created by its evasive character respecting Mr. Lincoln. The entire absence of eulogy of the slain President was remarked. There was no mention of his name or of his character, or of his office, the only allusion in any way whatever to Mr. Lincoln was Mr. Johnson's declaration that he 'was almost overwhelmed by the announcement of the sad event which has so recently occurred.'

"While he found no time to praise one whose praises were on every tongue, he made ample reference to himself and his own past history, and though speaking not more than five minutes, it was noticed that 'I' and 'my' and 'me' were used at least a score of times. A boundless egotism was inferred from the line of his remarks, 'My past public life, which has been long and laborious, has been founded, as I in good conscience believe, upon the great principle of right which lies at the base of all things.'

" 'I must be permitted to say, if I understand the feelings of my own heart, I have long labored to ameliorate and alleviate the conditions of the great mass of the American people.

" 'Toil and an honest advocacy of the great principles of free government have been my lot. The duties have been mine, the consequence God's.' "

Senator John P. Hale, of New Hampshire, who was present on this occasion, said, with characteristic wit, that—

"Johnson seemed willing to share the glory of his achievements with his Creator, but utterly forgot that Mr. Lincoln had any share or credit in the suppression of the rebellion."

Three days later, April 18, a delegation of distinguished citizens from Illinois called upon Mr. Johnson under circumstances extraordinary and most touching. The dead President still lay in the White House, before the solemn and august procession should leave the national Capitol to bear his mortal remains to the State which had loved and honored him. The delegation called to assure his successor of their respect and confidence, and in reply to Gov. Oglesby, the spokesman of the Illinois delegation, Mr. Johnson responded respecting the dead, President Lincoln, and with profound emotion of the tragical termination of Mr. Lincoln's life. He said:

"The beloved of all hearts has been assassinated." He then paused thoughtfully and added: "And when we trace this crime to its cause, when we remember the source from whence the assassin drew his inspiration, and then look at the result, we stand yet more astounded at this most barbarous, most diabolical act. Who can trace its cause through successive steps back to that source which is the spring of all our woes? No one can say that if the perpetrator of this fiendish deed be arrested he should not undergo the extremest penalty of the law known for crime. None can say that mercy should interpose. But is he alone guilty?"

I charge the reader in the light of the facts that have been written and the statement made by John St. Helen, that you compare this oration of Andrew Johnson over the body of Lincoln with that of Marc Antony over the dead body of Caesar.

The character and force of Mr. Johnson's words were anomalous and in many respects contradictory.

Mr. Blaine says of him in his "Twenty Years in Congress:" "Mr. Johnson by birth belonged. to that large class of people in the South known as the 'poor white.'" (Mr. Blaine should have said "Poor white trash," a term applied to a disreputable class of poor white people who would be equally unworthy and socially ostracised if rich. It was and is no disgrace in the South to be "poor," and no social ostracism extended to the poor, if honorable.)

"Many wise men regarded it as a fortunate circumstance that Mr. Lincoln's successor was from the South," says Mr. Blaine, "though a much larger number in the North found in this fact a source of disquietude, saying that Mr. Johnson had the misfortune of not possessing any close or intimate knowledge of the people of the loyal States; and it was found, moreover, that his relations with the ruling spirit of the South in the exciting period preceding the war specially unfitted him for harmonious co-operation with them in the pending exigencies. (Vol. II., page 3.)

"Mr. Johnson had been during his entire life a Democrat, and had attained complete control of the Democratic party in the State of Tennessee and had filled various official positions in the State, and finally that of Democratic United States Senator from the State of Tennessee." (Vol. II., page 4.)

I pass the above quotations without further comment than to challenge the thought of the reader to their significance to the political relations of Andrew Johnson with the Democratic politics of the State of Tennessee. In this connection I have sought to learn something, if possible, of Mr. Lincoln's feeling toward Vice-President Johnson, but find only a few sentences in written history touching their relations, which are recorded by William H. Herndon and Jesse W. Wierk, in their biography of the life of Lincoln, in Volume 2, at page 232, in which Mrs. Lincoln speaks as follows:

THE SEPARATION.

"My husband placed great confidence in my knowledge of human nature, and it was his intention to remove Seward as soon as peace was made in the South. He greatly disliked Andrew Johnson. On one occasion we noticed him following us and it displeased Mr. Lincoln so much that he turned and asked in a loud voice, 'Why is this man,' meaning Andrew Johnson, 'forever following me?'"

Thus we have conduct suspicious in its nature of Andrew Johnson toward Mr. Lincoln. And the world will ask of all mankind the same question Mr. Lincoln asked of his wife. And why was it that Andrew Johnson should have followed Mr. Lincoln? Does St. Helen's story explain Johnson's conduct— Johnson's motives?

In this connection it is interesting to know how Lincoln passed the last day of his life. Mrs. Lincoln says:

"He spent the last day of his life, the 14th day of April, 1865, by taking an early breakfast and attending a Cabinet meeting at 11 o'clock, at which Gen. Grant was present. He spent the afternoon with Gov. Oglesby, Senator Jones and other friends from Illinois."

On the afternoon of this day, in conversation with Mr. Colfax, only a short time before they should go to the theater, Mr. Lincoln invited Mr. Colfax to attend the theater with him, saying that he had secured a box at Ford's Theater for the purpose of entertaining Gen. Grant, but that Gen. Grant had just declined the invitation and had left the city, and that he (Lincoln) did not want the people entirely disappointed in their expectation of seeing both himself and Gen. Grant at the theater that evening, and would be glad to have Mr. Colfax accompany him, taking Gen. Grant's place. This Colfax declined.

It has always been an interesting question to me why, and how, under what conditions could Gen. Grant have been so successfully decoyed away from the City of Washington on so important an occasion, almost at the hour of attending this theater party in company with President Lincoln as the great Federal heroes of the civil war?

Gen. Grant, in explanation of the occurrence, says that late on the afternoon in question he received a note from his wife expressing some frivolous reasons as to why they should leave the city at once and visit their daughter, I believe, in Dubuque, Iowa. He says that on reaching Philadelphia he heard of the assassination of President Lincoln and returned at once by special train to Washington. These facts of history I likewise present to the public mind without comment. I trust, however, that I may be pardoned for saying here that I esteem my personal acquaintance with Gen. Grant an honor and a privilege and I now place myself on record in vindication of any thought or charge against the honor or integrity of character of this great man, and make mention of this incident only that the world may know the facts, as told me, of the actions and conduct of those whose names were in any way linked or associated with this story.

CHAPTER IX.

THE PURSUIT OF BOOTH

In the month of December, 1897, by some agency unknown to me, I found a copy of the Sunday edition of the Boston Globe, dated December 12, 1897, in the reception hall of my home. How this paper came to be in my home is unknown to me. I did not take it by subscription, nor have I or any member of my family ever, before or since, purchased a copy of the Boston Globe, nor has a copy of this paper at any other time been in my office or home. How this special paper came to my home is a complete mystery to myself and to every member of my household. My purpose is not to convey the idea that the presence of the Boston Globe was an intrusion in my home, for the contrary is true, because it was appreciated and read with great interest, and I regard it as worth many times its price as an entertainer for any household. I take pardonable pride in the State of Massachusetts and its people, for this State has been the home of my ancestors and kinsmen since the year 1635.

GEN. D. D. DANA.
Under Orders of Gen. C. C. Augur, Connected With the
Army at Washington. The Pursuer of John Wilkes Booth.

THE SURRATT TAVERN.

At Surrattville, Where Booth and Herold Stayed the Night of the 13th of April, 1865, as They Returned to Washington, and When Booth Waited for Herold to Overtake Him in His Flight.

The point is, by what mysterious means did this Sunday edition of the Boston Globe, containing the first published statement of Gen. D. D. Dana, of Lubec, Maine, giving a full account of his knowledge respecting the assassination of President Lincoln, and a detailed statement of his pursuit of John Wilkes Booth, twenty-three years after I had heard the story of John St. Helen, who claimed to be John Wilkes Booth. To my surprise the story of Gen. Dana corroborated in its minutest detail the story St. Helen told to me in his confession recounting Booth's escape from Washington, D. C., to the Garrett home, in Virginia.

David D. Dana, brother of Charles A. Dana, the founder, owner and publisher of the New York Sun, in December, 1897, lived in a small, one-story frame house in West Lubec, Maine. This being the ancestral home of his wife's people, where he settled some twenty years prior to December, 1897, at the time when the opening of lead mines in this section promised to make Lubec famous the world over, and after years of mining with indifferent success, Gen. Dana settled down to the quiet life of the farmer with his wife and many pets as companions, being eight miles from the nearest village. But he was by no means a recluse, being well informed on all current events, and a constant reader of the newspapers and periodicals of the day.

Gen. Dana's story is given in full below:

"The Boston Sunday Globe, Dec. 12, 1897.

"HE ALMOST SAVED LINCOLN.

"David Dana, Brother of Chas. A. Dana, Tried to Prevent the Assassination of the Martyr President—Now a Dweller in Lubec, Maine—He Tells of His Pursuit of Booth.

"Away down in a remote corner of New England, in the most easterly town in this broad country, dwells the man who alone had knowledge beforehand of the meditated assassination of Lincoln, and who tried by every means in his power to thwart the conspiracy, but all in vain.

"This man, David Dana, brother of the late Chas. A. Dana, is a most unique and interesting character, and one who has seen his full share of life, and has been a part of the most stirring events in our coun-

94

try's history. It was the writer's good fortune recently to hear him tell of the part he took in the pursuit of the assassin, Booth, and his accomplice, Herold. Inasmuch as the story gives facts never before laid before the public, the recital cannot fail to be of great interest to every one who has ever perused the story of these exciting times.

" 'In the spring of '65 I was near Washington,' began Mr. Dana, 'with my headquarters at Fort Baker, just above the east branch of the Potomac. It was within the lines of the Third Brigade of Harden's Division, Twenty-second Corps, commanded by Gen. C. C. Augur, under whom I was provost marshal. I had authority over nearly all those parts of Maryland lying between the east branch of the Potomac and the Patuxent river. This part of the State was swarming with rebels, and I was commissioned to watch all their movements and learn if possible of any plots against the Federal government.

" 'While patrolling this territory I learned that a plot was forming against the government, and that the blow would undoubtedly be aimed against the life of President Lincoln. I at once asked for a battalion of veteran cavalry, in addition to the regular provost guard, and the request was granted. I was ordered to establish a line of pickets from Fort

Meigs on the left to Geisboro point on the right, with orders to permit none to enter the city of Washington during the day unless they could give their names, where they were from, and what was their business at the Capitol.

" 'From sundown to sunrise no one was to enter or leave the city except in case of sickness or death. All suspicious persons were arrested and sent to the commanding general for examination.

"On Friday, April 14, 1865, two men appeared before the guard on the road leading into Washington from the east. Refusing to give their names or state their business, they were arrested and put in the guard tent, whence they were to be sent to headquarters. ᵧThis was about 1 o'clock in the afternoon. In an hour or two they gave their names as Booth and Herold.

" 'The officers on guard under me carried out my orders so strictly that it was very annoying to the rebel sympathizers who wished access to the city, so that many complaints were made by prominent citizens of Maryland.

" 'About 4 p.m. I received an order from Gen. Augur to release all prisoners held by the guards and to withdraw the guard until further orders. I sent an orderly to the officers on the line from Fort Meigs easterly, with orders to release all prisoners and to report to me at Fort Baker. On the line from Fort Meigs to Surrattville I went in person and withdrew the guard to my headquarters.

" 'Booth and Herold were released as soon as the orders reached the guard, and they proceeded at once to Washington, reaching there about 6:30 in the afternoon. I had a guard at each end of the bridge on the eastern branch of the Potomac and one of the guards knew Booth and recognized him as he rode into the city and as he came out after the assassination, and had it been known that he had killed Lincoln escape would have been impossible.

" 'I returned to headquarters about 11 p. m. and had dismissed the guard and was eating supper, when an officer rode into camp with the startling intelligence that Lincoln was killed and that the murderer, with another man, had ridden at a rapid pace into the country.

" 'I called out the guard and sent detachments in different directions and then went to the bridge to learn what I could there. On my way I met a company of cavalry, the 13th New York, which I ordered to patrol the river to Guisi Point and learn all they could and then return to Fort Baker.

" 'At the bridge I found an orderly from Gen. Augur with orders for me to report to him at Washington without delay. I did so, and was ushered into his presence, where I found him standing by his desk with streaming eyes.

" 'My God, marshal,' he cried, upon seeing me, 'if I had listened to your advice this terrible thing never would have happened!'

" 'After conversing with him for a few moments I was appointed adjutant general on his staff and ordered to use my own judgment as to the best way of capturing Booth. The order read as follows:

" 'To Commanders of all Divisions, Brigades, Regiments, Companies, and Posts: You will obey all orders emanating from Adjt. Gen. and Provost Marshall D. D. Dana the same as though especially issued from these headquarters.

(Signed) Maj. Gen. C. C. Augur, Commanding 22d Corps in Dept. of Washington.'

" 'While with Gen. Augur and by his request I laid out the plan for the capture of Booth. First, one of the swifest steamers which could be obtained should patrol the Potomac as far as the Patuxent river and seize all boats which could not give a good account of themselves. Then a steamer should be sent up the Patuxent and all boats on this river were to be seized at all hazards to as far as Horse Head ferry.

" 'These orders were telegraphed to the boats on the Patuxent and were carried out to the letter. The reason was this: In scouting through Maryland I had learned that a boat would be used by the assassin, who would go by land to the Patuxent, thence across to the Albert river, from there to the Atlantic coast, and thence to Mexico. The only thing that prevented Booth's escape was the seizure of these boats.

" 'I returned to Fort Baker, left orders for the cavalry, who were out scouting, took a small detachment of my own guard and started after Booth, taking the road by Surrattville to Bryantown. As we passed by the Surratt mansion all was as dark as though it had never been inhabited, but I found an old man and woman who had a boy sick with the smallpox. Finding that no information could be obtained there, from the old man or his wife, I took him along with us for a mile and a half to a secluded dell. Refusing to give the desired information, I ordered him to be strung up to the limb of a big oak tree.

" 'It was a clear night with the moon just rising, its silvery glints touching the tops of the trees in the dell and the flickering light of the campfire, which the men had kindled, casting fantastic shadows here and there. The rope was made fast about the old man's neck and, at a signal from me, he was hoisted up and suspended between heaven and earth.

It was a weird and gruesome scene, there in the light of the fire and moon was the swaying body of the man struggling in his futile efforts to grasp the rope, while the spasmodic action of his body and the gurgling sounds from his throat produced an effect never to be forgotten.

" 'I ordered him to be cut down after a few moments and he was resuscitated. Rather than try a second pull on the rope he told me that Booth and Herold had been at the Surratt mansion and had had something to eat and drink and that after supper, though Booth was badly hurt, they had mounted their horses and rode toward Bryantown.

" 'I pushed on after them and a few miles from Bryantown I came to a detachment of ten men under a sergeant as patrol guard to watch suspicious people in that section. I sent the sergeant to Port Tobacco at once, and ordered the troops to scout up the Patuxent river to arrest all suspicious persons and to report to me at Bryantown. The patrol guard afterward acknowledged that they heard the clatter of Booth's and Herold's horses' feet as they passed by on the road leading to Dr. Samuel Mudd's toward Bryantown.

" 'This came about from the fact that a short distance above the guard was a road leading to Dr. Mudd's, who resided about three and a half miles from the village, and this road the pair had taken, reaching the doctor's house about 4 a. m., about two hours ahead of my troops.

" 'I arrived at Bryantown about 6 o'clock, and at once placed guards at all the roads leading into the village, with orders that anyone might enter the town but that none were to leave it. About 2 o'clock that afternoon the detachment of troops from Port Tobacco reached me. In the meantime troops had been sent to Woodbine ferry and Horsehead ferry, all the boats had been seized and all crossing of the river had been stopped.

" 'By taking possession of these positions and seizing the ferry boats and by closely guarding the line of the river Booth's chances of escape this way were cut off. Could he have got across the Patuxent river into Calvert county, he would most certainly have reached Mexico in safety.

" 'After Booth and Herold arrived at Dr. Mudd's Booth's leg was set, and after giving them their breakfast, the doctor made a crutch for Booth and fixed him up ready to start at an instant's notice.

" 'Dr. Mudd came into Bryantown at 2 o'clock in the afternoon and stayed there until 8 or 9 in the evening, when a cousin of his, Dr. George Mudd, asked as a personal favor, a pass for him through the lines. After closely questioning Samuel Mudd and believing him to know nothing of Booth, and having confidence in what his cousin said, I let Dr. Samuel Mudd go.

" 'During the doctor's long absence Booth got uneasy and sent Herold on horseback to Bryantown. Learning that troops were in the town, he tied his horse to a large clump of willows that grew on the side of a stream near the road, and there watched for Dr. Mudd's return.

" 'When the doctor made his appearance Herold came out and the two returned to the doctor's house. Booth was anxious to leave at once, but the good doctor assured him that there was no danger that night.

" 'George Mudd, let me say in passing, never intimated to me that his friend was a doctor, or was a relative of his. I learned the next day, when it was too late, that his cousin was a rank rebel, and I plainly told George Mudd what I thought of him.

" 'The fugitives left Dr. Mudd's early the next morning and took the road for Horsehead ferry. When within two and one-half miles of the ferry they saw a man of about sixty years leaning on a fence in front of his house; Booth rode up and asked him if he had heard the news of Lincoln being killed. He said yes, he had heard it from some troops that had arrived at the ferry. Booth asked him if there were any troops then at Horsehead ferry and the man told him there were.

" 'Booth got a drink of water and wanted a drink of whiskey, but the old man had none. He asked the men who they were, and Booth answered: "Detectives looking for Booth and Herold." "What are you doing with a crutch?" was the rejoinder.

" 'The assassin explained that his horse had stumbled and had fallen upon him, hurting his leg very badly. They asked the way to Woodbine ferry, and being directed, set off at a brisk trot.

" 'When within two miles of Woodbine ferry they met an old darkey and inquired: "How far is it to the ferry?" Upon being told they asked him the news. "Massa Lincum's killed an' Woodbine ferry's chock full of troops." "How many, uncle?" asked Booth. "Golly, massa, dere's more'n a hundred! Dey's swarming like bees!" answered the negro.

" 'The horsemen rode on a short distance through a gate into a mowing field, and there all trace of their horses' footprints were lost. But they returned to the vicinity of Dr. Mudd's and entered the Sekiah swamp from the east, where they spent two days and two nights, being supplied with food by friends near by.

" 'I had made arrangements for a detachment of troops to scour the swamp with a guide, when a

heavy storm came up and made it impossible. Had
I done so I certainly would have caught them, as
they did not leave until 2 or 3 o'clock that day.
When my troops reached the island the next day
they found where the horses had been tethered, and
the very moss where Booth and Herold had slept.
They also found the pieces of blanket with which
their horses' hoofs had been muffled. How they
made their way from Woodbine ferry to the swamp
is a mystery. It could only have been done by wrap-
ping the horses' feet in blankets.

" 'The different movements they made from the
time of the assassination to their reaching Sekiah
swamp shows that they had their course all laid out
beforehand. They knew where to go and who their
friends were and were only prevented from escaping by the rapid movements of the troops under my
command.

" 'Sekiah swamp lies a short distance nearly west
of Bryantown. It is full of quagmires and sinkholes
and is exceedingly dangerous to enter except by day-
time. Even then great caution is required unless
a person is acquainted with the swamp. Booth and
Herold must have had a guide both going in and
coming out.

" 'They never could have got their horses there alone; to attempt it would have been the last of them.

" 'There is a small stream running through the swamp, but large enough to float a small boat. It discharges into the Patuxent river. After leaving the swamp the fugitives went to a log cabin in a thick growth of pines and underbrush quite distant from any road. It was the dwelling of a man named Jones, who had a negress for a housekeeper. It was in that scrubby pine and underbrush, back of the house, that the two horses were killed and buried.

"Here Booth and Herold were kept three or four days, when they were taken by boat down the outlet of the swamp to a point below where the troops were stationed, and from there they were carried in a wagon to a point on the Patuxent nearly opposite Aquia creek. From here they were taken across the Potomac and made their way to Garrett's near Bowling Green, where Booth was killed.' "

A Bay State soldier corroborates in part the story of Gen. David A. Dana, as well as that of St. Helen. This soldier was stationed at the bridge crossing the East Potomac river, on the road leading into Washington, which John Wilkes Booth crossed going into Washington City and again on his return after the assassination the evening of the same day. This man is Mr. F. A. Demond, and I give his letter in full:

"Mr. D. D. Dana:

"Dear Sir and Comrade—I was very much interested in reading your account of how you tried to prevent the assassination of the late President Lincoln, as published in The Globe of yesterday. It brought back old memories to me of away back in '64, as I was a member of your old provost guard, with headquarters at Fort Baker.

"Well do I remember those days. I was detailed from my company—Co. C., Capt. A. W. Brigham, then stationed at Fort Mahan—and ordered to report to you at Fort Baker for duty on provost guard. I did so, and was employed guarding prisoners, sawing wood and going down to Uniontown searching for soldiers without passes. After a short time of service at headquarters I, with some others from your command, was sent to guard the bridge leading from Washington to Uniontown, down by the navy yard.

"I was stationed at the Uniontown end of the bridge where the gates were hung to stop people from going to Washington. I was under the orders of Corp. Sullivan—I think that was his name—and the command at the other end of the bridge, the Washington side, was under Sergt. Cobb.

106

THE PURSUIT OF BOOTH.

"I was present the night that Booth and Herold crossed after Booth had shot the President, but was not on post. I stood in the door of the block house when Booth rode up and heard him ask the guard if anyone had gone through lately. I heard the guard on the post answer him, 'No,' and ask him what he was doing out there this time of night?

"He made some kind of answer about going to see some one who lived out on the T. B. road. I did not pay much attention at this time to what they were talking about. I helped open the gate and he rode through.

"A short time after this Herold rode over the bridge and asked if there had been anyone through mounted on a bay horse. Upon being told that there had, he muttered something about being a pretty man not to wait for him.

"Well, we opened the gate and let him through and he rode off in a hurry. About twenty minutes later, I should say, we heard a great uproar across the bridge and in a short time got word of the assassination. If we had only known it sooner neither one of them would have passed us, as I would have shot them as quickly as I would a mad dog. But it was too late; they were out of sight and hearing by that time.

"I remember when you came down to meet someone that was waiting on the Washington side, but never knew who it was until I read the account given by you in The Sunday Globe. I remember of your going in pursuit, and, if I am not mistaken, one of Co. C.'s boys, Charles Joise, was with you.

"Excuse my writing to you, but I was so glad to hear from you, Lieutenant, that I had to let you know that one of your old boys was still living. Hoping sometime to see you on a visit to me up here, I remain, yours with great respect,

"F. A. Demond, Cavendish, Vt.

"Late private Co. C., Third Heavy Artillery, Massachusetts Volunteers."

It will be observed that the statements made by Gen. D. D. Dana, supported by the letter of Mr. F. A. Demond, corroborate the statements and confessions made to me by John St. Helen (claiming himself to be Booth) more than twenty-five years previous to Dana's publication. That the statements of Gen. Dana and St. Helen, or Booth, should differ in immaterial details is not surprising, but the main points agree—that is, St. Helen says, he (Booth) and Herold were returning to Washington City on the morning of April 14th, 1865; that they were arrested and detained at the block house located at the bridge over the east branch of the Potomac; that they were released and went into Washington from this bridge;

that Booth was recognized at the time of his de-
tention at the East Potomac bridge; that after the
assassination of President Lincoln Booth and Herold returned over the same route over which they
came into the city, crossing the East Potomac bridge,
which is also the route leading to Uniontown, mentioned by Demond; that in crossing said bridge and
passing the guards they used the pass words ''T.
B.,' or ''T. B. Road.'' It is undeniably a fact that
Booth is corroborated in his statements that arrangements had been made for his escape; that he did
escape from Washington through the Federal lines,
is confessedly true, though the city was completely
surrounded and guarded by the 22d Army Corps,
composed of many thousands of union men, an army
within itself, charged with the duty of protecting
the City of Washington and guarding the life of
President Lincoln against danger, which Dana says
he knew was threatened, and he had known it for
months prior to the President's assassination.

In comparing the statements of St. Helen, or
Booth, with that of Gen. Dana, made twenty or twenty-five years after the occurrences, we find that Gen.
Dana's statement published in the city of Boston in
1897, is almost a verbatim copy of that made by St.
Helen to me in the State of Texas, though more than
two thousand miles of territory divided them and a

difference in time of some years intervened. These statements could not have been preconcerted, and because of these conditions, each corroborating the other, the accounts of the affair bear the stamp of physical truth.

The reader will not fail to note with anxious concern, and demand explanation of the statement of Gen. Dana, when he says:

"The life of the President (Lincoln) was then (on the 14th day of April, 1865) known to be in imminent and impending danger, and so well was this known to him and others, that he asked and obtained an extra force of mounted men to better guard the life of the President (Lincoln), and the lines of protection had been tightened around Washington City in every precautionary way, looking to the safety of the life of the President, then threatened. Being thus forewarned, forearmed and fully prepared to guard against a danger known to him, why was it that without a change in these conditions, the life of the President still threatened, without increase of hope for his safety, or promised immunity, rumored or otherwise, danger to which the commanding officer, Major Gen. C. C. Augur, and himself, Gen. Dana, were admittedly advised of, John Wilkes Booth, the assassin, a known Southern sympathizer who constitute one of the class of men from whom the officers expected the attempted assault on the President with the purpose of taking his life, of which they had been warned, was permitted to enter the city less than eight hours before the assassination under his own name of John Wilkes Booth? And Herold, Booth's accomplice, was also permitted to enter with him. They entered the city in such a manner as to cause suspicion of their conduct and purpose, were arrested and detained for a number of hours at the East Potomac bridge. Yet they were permitted to leave the city, returning over the very bridge where they had been held prisoners only eight hours before. They approached the bridge under circumstances that should have excited suspicion, the same suspicious characters who had been detained but a few hours before, and yet were permitted to pass the guards without arrest by simply giving the pass word ''T. B.'' or ''T. B. Road,'' which was meaningless, unless understood by the guard on duty.

It will be remembered that Gen. Dana says that the strictest orders had been given to the guards to permit no one to pass at night, except on account of sickness or death, and that all suspicious characters were to be arrested and sent to headquarters to be examined by the commanding officer, Gen. C. C. Augur. If these orders were to be carried out by the

111

guards they were violated because it was night and the reason given by Booth to pass out was neither sickness or death. It can not be denied that the approach of Booth and Herold to this bridge, from the city about ten thirty o'clock at night, their horses under full spur, at a high rate of speed, necessarily created suspicion in the minds of the guards, under circumstances to be remembered. Booth, a suspicious character, first approached, giving the words "T. B.," or "T. B. Road," and was passed, while Herold, also a suspicious character it seems, passed the guards by simply inquiring if a man had passed, and describing Booth. A few minutes later, coming in hot pursuit, the livery man and owner of the horse ridden by Herold reached the bridge, chasing Herold and just behind him, was stopped and made to tell his purpose, which was:

That he wanted to overtake Herold, who was riding away with his horse; that the President had been shot and that Booth and Herold were guilty and were escaping. It seems that this excuse was not sufficient for the guard on duty, and the owner of the horse, the leader of the chase after the escaping criminals, was turned back. (This was the commotion of which Mr. Demond speaks when they learned of the shooting of President Lincoln and the incident mentioned by Secretary John Hay in his public utterance when referring to the passing of Booth and Herold over the bridge and the pursuit of the owner of the horse ridden by Herold, when he says, "Booth and Herold were permitted to pass and the only honest man who sought to pass was stopped.")

In this connection we have no information from history or Gen. Dana, from whom such information should come, that the guard who allowed Booth and Herold to pass was disciplined for the violation of orders. It, therefore, stands to reason that the guard was not punished but was simply carrying out orders in passing Booth, and Herold his accomplice, and also in refusing to allow others to pass. But is the situation explained by Gen. Dana, who says that the orders prohibited the passing of persons through the lines, except upon conditions mentioned, and that he had individually taken in the guards at the East Potomac bridge, which he had not.

The question is, what interest did he have—or why should Dana individually do this, and intrust his orders at all other points to be delivered by an orderly? What special interest, I ask, should Dana have had in this identical spot, through which Booth was later to escape when he had killed President Lincoln?

Gen. Dana, himself, confesses that he went to the East Potomac bridge and gave his orders in person. And, again, I ask, What were those orders? History does not record. He does not say. The only answer is the act of the guard. Let the world interpret what those orders were. It is true, because it was a physical fact, the guard was on duty—Booth was allowed to pass on giving the pass word "T. B.;" Herold, his accomplice, was allowed to pass. Was the guard obeying orders when he allowed Booth and Herold to pass and turned back "the only honest man," the man in pursuit? If this act of the guard was a violation of orders he was caught red-handed and should have been punished as a particeps criminis for the crime of the assassination of President Lincoln. The penalty for which, under the order of Secretary Stanton of April 20th, 1865, making all those who aided Booth in his escape guilty of his (Booth's) crime, was punishable by death. Then, I ask, why was not this punishment meted out to the men who alone had it in their power to prevent the escape of Booth and Herold, but who did, knowingly, permit them to escape?

Further, Gen. Dana says that the orders were for calling in the guards to his headquarters, located at Fort Baker, and that he individually gave the orders at the East Potomac bridge; that these orders

114

were issued to him (Dana) about four o'clock in the afternoon of April 14th, 1865, by Gen. C. C. Augur.

The reader is asked to note the significance of the fact that at about this hour St. Helen (Booth) says that he and Vice-President Johnson had separated at the Kirkwood hotel, Johnson going to arrange for Booth's escape. Is this order to Dana from his superior commanding officer, Major Gen. C. C. Augur, an echo of Johnson's mission?

Again, Gen. Dana says that in pursuance to these orders the guards were removed to his headquarters at Fort Baker. But it is a physical fact that at ten thirty o'clock p. m., when Booth crossed the bridge, the guards had not been removed; and if removed at all it was done after this as a subterfuge for carrying out the order to call in the guards, which seems to have been the case. For true it is that Gen. Dana says he had not reached his headquarters with this guard until about eleven o'clock p. m. that night and was eating his evening meal when he first received word of the shooting of the President.

Any one knowing the distance from the East Potomac bridge to Fort Baker will readily understand how Gen. Dana, together with his guards, mounted and leaving the East Potomac bridge at about ten thirty o'clock could reach Fort Baker at or about eleven o'clock. This would make the statements of Gen. Dana consistent, and this I believe to be a correct explanation of his seeming contradiction in respect to the matter of withdrawing the guards from the East Potomac bridge, which responsibility he personally assumed and for which he will be held responsible.

However this may be, it is true that the guards were on duty at the bridge and, as a matter of fact and of history, whether intentionally or unintentionally, did assist Booth and his accomplice in passing the line, and equally true that they did refuse to allow the owner of the horse ridden by Herold to pass a few minutes later. Then, I ask, why this discrimination against the man in pursuit of the fleeing assassin and his accomplice? This can only be answered by the guards, or Gen. Dana. Unless the conduct of the guards explains. But, legally holding these men responsible for the necessary consequence of their acts, they did aid Booth in his escape, while all the circumstances attendant upon Booth's passing of the guards tend to establish their guilty knowledge, or the guilty knowledge and conduct of their superior officers.

At this eleventh hour, while he was yet at his meal, Gen. Dana says he was ordered before Gen. C. C. Augur, but then too late, as the crime had been already committed and the assassin had escaped the confines of the military powers of Washington.

Gen. Dana, on reaching the headquarters of Gen. Augur, found him in tears and his first words were: "My God, marshal, if I had listened to your advice this terrible thing would never have happened."

I ask, and the civilized world listens for the reply —What had Gen. Dana advised Gen. Augur touching the safety of the President, and "this terrible thing," as he calls it, prior to the assassination, which, in Gen. Augur's opinion, if heeded, would have prevented the killing of President Lincoln? Is this a self-accusation—an unwitting admission of his responsibility for the death of President Lincoln? This expression of self-accusation, taken in connection with Gen. Augur's surprising and unexplained order, issued about four o'clock on April 14th, 1865, in face of the known and impending danger to the life of President Lincoln, is startling. The withdrawing of the guard from the protection of the President on the late afternoon of the evening of his assassination has never been explained. And the bloody deed was accomplished in less than six hours after the order of withdrawal was issued, and before the ink was well dry on the record which changed the policy of the government for the protection of the life of the President, long guarded by

117

a well-maintained standing army at Washington, and made possible the escape of the assassin. Without reason, without explanation and without request, and without suggestion even, of the President, or any other person in authority in the army superior in command to Gen. C. C. Augur, this important move was made, changing the fixed plans and tearing down the barriers of protection so long deemed necessary by the government as a wise and prudential policy, upon the authority and orders only of Gen. C. C. Augur, so far as we are informed by Gen. Dana.

In the light of events following this mysterious order, we ask, to what conduct of his or advice of Gen. Dana could Major Gen. C. C. Augur refer as his failure to listen to Gen. Dana? Could it have been that Dana had advised the holding of Booth and Herold while they were yet prisoners at the block house, at the East Potomac bridge? Or had he, against the advice or knowledge of Gen. Dana, entered into the plans of conspiracy against the life of President Lincoln?

One would infer from the statements imputed to him by Gen. Dana that Major Gen. Augur had had it in his power, and was so advised by Gen. Dana, to save the life of the President and had failed to do so and that. too, against the admonitions of Gen.

Dana, to which he (Augur) had declined to listen, according to his own confession.

This leads to the conclusion that Gen. Augur must have known of a purpose to take the life of President Lincoln previous to the assassination; otherwise he could not have prevented it by taking the advice of Gen. Dana. According to Dana's statement Gen. Augur admits that he could have prevented the commission of an act by another. Unless Gen. Augur had knowledge of the purpose to commit that act, and of the person who was to perform the specific act complained of, he had no such power as he admitted. Therefore, upon the statement of Gen. Dana, which we assume to be true, Major Gen. C. C. Augur had a knowledge of some act, which, if performed, would have saved the life of President Lincoln. Reasoning from the assumed admission to physical facts, based upon the proviso that Gen. Dana is correctly reporting, which I believe to be true because his report of the pursuit of Booth is in the main a strong corroboration of the story of St. Helen (or Booth) told to me, this is the inevitable conclusion, applying the legal rule, the standard by which we measure the words of men—if true in one thing, true in all, or false in one thing, false in all. This rule must sustain the statements of Dana, which, without further explanation, must

"My God, marshal, if I had taken your advice this terrible thing would not have happened."

(how that Major Gen. Augur, on his own confession, could have saved the life of President Lincoln, but did not do it, even when advised to do so by Gen. Dana, his subordinate officer, and conscience-whipped after the assassination he cries out:

And shall these words ring on and on through the changing cycles of time, a lasting tribute to the truth of the old, trite saying, "Murder will out" and "truth, though crushed to the earth, will rise again?"

GEN. C. C. AUGUR.

Commander of the Army Stationed Around Washington for
Protection of the Life of Lincoln, and the Home of the
Government, Who Issued the Order Calling in the
Guards.

MRS. SURRATT

And Her Boarding-house in Washington City, Where Booth
Met Her Son, John H. Surratt, Delivering the Letter From
David E. Herold, Their Mutual Friend.

CHAPTER X.

THE EAST POTOMAC BRIDGE

Gen. Dana says, in speaking of the pursuit of Booth and Herold: "Booth and Herold remained a day and one night at the home of Dr. Samuel Mudd." St. Helen (or Booth) told me they reached the home of Dr. Mudd just before daylight on the morning of April 15th, 1865, the morning after the assassination, where his riding boot was cut off by Dr. Mudd and his sprained ankle and fractured shin bone dressed and splintered by the doctor with parts of a cigar box, and the old doctor made him a rough crutch out of a broom handle; when after an early breakfast, their horses in the brush near by, having finished feeding, they, thanking and paying Dr. Mudd for his services, mounted their horses and left, riding the most direct way they could, keeping well in the country and by-roads, to the home of Mr. Cox, during the 15th day of April, 1865, the day after the killing of President Lincoln, showing substantial corroboration of Gen. Dana so far.

Gen. Dana says Booth and Herold killed their horses while they were in hiding back of the Cox plantation on the Potomac river, but Booth says the horses were not killed but taken away, as he supposed, by Mr. Jones.

That this is true, I am inclined to believe, for two reasons: First, the horse ridden by Booth and described to me by St. Helen (or Booth) was a very fine and valuable animal, purchased by him in Maryland some time before this event. The second reason is that Gen. Dana's men were too close on Booth and Herold to permit of their killing the horses, which must have been done by shooting them. Dana then says they were buried. This would have been a physical impossibility, for Booth, in his crippled condition, could not help and Herold was without the necessary implements with which to do it.

Booth says the Federal troops of cavalry were so close to them in their hiding in the pine brush behind the Cox plantation that they could hear the footfalls of the horses and the voices of the men, and for that reason their horses were taken away to prevent their neighs from attracting attention to them by the passing Cavalry, as they "had neighed frequently, much to our fear and discomfort."

Gen. Dana further says that "Booth and Herold must have had guides." The truth is Herold was well acquainted with this section of the country, as was Booth, from his previous inspections of this

route over which Lincoln was to have been carried
if kidnaped and taken to Richmond, as originally
designed. It is true, however, that Herold was to
some extent a guide for Booth.

Herold is dead and I suppose I am the only living man who knows why Booth became associated
with Herold, so unlike and inferior to himself, for
David E. Herold was seemingly a man of no cultivation, and was a drug clerk employed in a drug store
in Washington City, where he made the acquaintance of Booth.

The explanation made to me by St. Helen (or
Booth) was that he had become acquainted with
Herold while he was a clerk in a drug store which
he (Booth) frequented to buy cosmetics sometimes
used by him in his or others' makeup for the stage.
And at these meetings he learned of Herold's old
acquaintance with this section of the country,
what was then called "The underground route between Washington, D. C., and Richmond, Virginia,"
and for this reason he made a friend of Herold and
took him into his confidence. It was in company
with Herold that Booth made his first as well as
many other trips over this route. In the meantime
he learned that Herold knew John H. Surratt. Having found Herold a willing and loyal friend, desir-
ous of lending himself to Booth's plans against the

Federal government and the life of President Lincoln, Booth trusted him; and it will be remembered that it was Herold who gave Booth the letter of introduction to John H. Surratt.

Mrs. Surratt, the most prominent of the persons suspected of complicity in Booth's crime, was innocent of any complicity whatever in the matter; was a woman of middle age at the time of her execution, rather good-looking, and the mother of two or more children, among them John H. Surratt and a daughter. Mrs. Surratt was at one time comfortably well off but had been reduced to the necessity of removing from Surrattville, her home, to Washington, where she kept a boarding house on H street. I am informed that Mrs. Surratt is the only woman ever hanged by a judgment of a Federal Adjudication.

Recurring to the incident at the East Potomac bridge and the statements made by Demond to Gen. Dana, where he says, "I well remember when you came down to meet some one that was waiting on the Washington side, but never knew who it was until I read the account given by you in The Sunday Globe."

Is this statement suggestive? Gen. Dana fails to mention that he had a meeting with some third party who was waiting for him at the East Potomac bridge on the Washington side.

Was this meeting by prearrangement? And does it explain why Gen. Dana went in person to the East Potomac bridge, ostensibly to call in the guard, but presumably to meet this party in waiting? We reach this conclusion from the physical fact that he did meet this party and that he did not call in the guards, if so, not until Booth had made good his escape.

Gen. Dana says that he went in person to the East Potomac bridge to call in the guard, using this language: "On the line from Fort Meigs to Surrattville I went in person and withdrew my guard to my headquarters," his headquarters being at Fort Baker. He follows this statement by saying: "I returned to headquarters about eleven o'clock that night and had dismissed my guards." Thus referring to, or meaning, the guards which he had called in from the East Potomac bridge, the point where Booth crossed the river.

Booth killed the President about ten minutes past ten o'clock p. m. and arrived at the East Potomac and crossed the bridge about ten thirty o'clock. Gen. Dana says he received the order to call in the guards about four o'clock that afternoon; that he went in person to call in the guards from this bridge; that he reached his headquarters at Fort Baker and dismissed his guards about eleven o'clock that night. Gen. Dana gives no account of himself from four o'clock p. m. until about eleven o'clock p. m. of the 14th day of April, 1865. Nothing of what he did at the bridge, what time he reached there, or when he left. Nothing of who this third party was at the bridge waiting on the Washington side, with whom he was seen to meet and talk by Demond.

Where was Gen. Dana when President Lincoln was shot? Of this he gives no account. Where was he when Booth and Herold crossed the bridge about ten thirty o'clock? Of this time he gives no account. Was he present at the bridge? He says he withdrew the guards, and the guards were present when Booth and Herold crossed!

Gen. Dana says: "I withdrew my guards to my headquarters and had dismissed them and was eating my evening meal at about eleven o'clock, when I heard the President was shot." Certainly Gen. Dana was not at his headquarters at the usual hour for taking meals.

If it be true that Dana withdrew the guards from the bridge it was certainly done after Booth and Herold had passed, for it is a physical fact that the guards were there when they passed over, so that the logical conclusion is that if the guard left at all they left after Booth and Herold had crossed the bridge.

Gen. Dana shows that when he arrived at the headquarters of Major Gen. Augur that Gen. Augur gave Dana complete command of all the forces to pursue and capture Booth. And we ask, is it not a significant fact that Gen. Dana should have misdirected all the troops which he sent out other than a single detachment, in pursuit of Booth, unless he knew the direction Booth had gone? Is it not strange that he himself, with a detail of men, without hesitation and without other information than such as he possessed before the shooting of President Lincoln— in fact, as if by intuition, took the proper trail by leaving Washington directly for Surrattville, crossing the East Potomac bridge as Booth and Herold had done, following along the trail in the wake of Booth and Herold, who arrived at the home of Dr. Mudd about four o'clock a. m., while Gen. Dana turned from the road leading to Dr. Mudd's home and went to Bryantown, just three and a half miles from Dr. Mudd's home, reaching Bryantown at six o'clock a. m., while Booth and Herold were yet at the home of the doctor. Dr. Mudd administered to Booth's pains, then went to Bryantown, where he called on Gen. Dana, and was permitted to leave Bryantown by Gen. Dana, as the general says, ''at the request of his cousin, Dr. George Mudd.'·

We ask, are these findings of fact mere incidents of the occasion? Shall we say it is entirely reasonable so to conclude?

Gen. Dana, in commenting on the Dr. Mudd incident, says: "George Mudd, let me say in passing, never intimated to me that his friend was a doctor, or was a relative of his. I learned this the next day when it was too late (as usual he does not explain how he found it out) that his cousin was a rank rebel, and I plainly told George Mudd what I thought of him."

Which we suggest must have been a great punishment to Dr. George Mudd and was quite the act of a hero on the part of Gen. Dana to thus occupy his time—reading lectures to Dr. George Mudd while in hot pursuit of and on the trail of the assassin of the President of the United States.

Thus spending his time at Bryantown, neglecting to go with his troops, or send them to capture Dr. Samuel Mudd at his home only three and a half miles away, in order that he might investigate the suspicious and offending conduct of Dr. Samuel Mudd, he, instead, sends a detachment of his troops with a guide to scour a nearby swamp looking for Booth and Herold, when a heavy storm came up and made it impossible to proceed with the search and the next day it was too late. As usual, convenient for Booth and Herold.

Thus practically ended Gen. Dana's chase after Booth at Bryantown.

Realizing that he was hunted with a zeal beyond the zeal prompting the searchers in following the ordinary criminal and bringing him to justice; stimulated by a burning desire for vengeance for the crime that startled the whole world, no less than the hope of the magnificent reward, which meant a fortune in those days, John Wilkes Booth decided to cast his lot among the Indians. He met many of the tribes and mingled with them, finally becoming associated with the Apache tribe, whose chief he described as being a man of docility, lazy and devoid of ambition. The males of the tribe, who are called bucks, were active and possessed of more than ordinary intelligence; the squaws, some of them pretty and attractive, were the slaves of the men. But, though these people were kind to him and his safety was absolutely secure among them, Booth could not accustom himself to the habits and customs of these rude people and the longing for kindred companionship drew him back again to the haunts of civilized man.

He went to Nebraska City, Nebraska, where he met and was entertained by a Mr. Treadkell, who

employed him later as a teamster, under the name
of Jesse Smith, in the fall of the year, 1866.   Mr.
Treadkell had a contract with the United States
government for hauling overland the supplies to the
United States army located at Salt Lake City, Utah.

In speaking of Booth Mr. Treadkell said: ''There
was always a strange thing about Jesse Smith, or
Booth. While he was a good driver of mules four in
hand, he did not have the slightest knowledge of
how to harness his team nor even how to hitch them
to the wagon.   But he was the life of the camp at
night and rendered himself so agreeable that I never
once thought of discharging him for his ignorance
in this respect, that he never was able to hitch up
his own team.   The other drivers were always gladly
willing to do this service for him and I myself would
much rather do this than give him up, on account
of his ability to entertain us at night.   He would
recite Shakespeare's plays, poems, etcetera, and tell
of his travels, which seemed to have been extensive.
His recitations were grandly eloquent.''

The day before reaching Salt Lake City and the
army officials Jesse Smith (Booth) left the wagon
and his employer, disappearing without notice or
compensation, according to Mr. Treadkell's statement, which corroborates St. Helen's (Booth) ver-
sion of the same story.   And I suppose he continued

his journey west to San Francisco where he met his mother and brother, Junius Brutus Booth.

A few years later Mr. Treadkell purchased a book containing the story of the assassination of President Lincoln and a picture of John Wilkes Booth the assassin, from which picture he was greatly surprised to recognize in his mysterious teamster, Jesse Smith, no less a person than John Wilkes Booth.

CHAPTER XI.

THE HAND OF SECRETARY STANTON

The government for some reason took up the pursuit of Booth independent of the movements of Gen Dana and the Army of Washington within the lines of the 3rd Brigade of Harden's Division, 22d Corps, commanded by Maj. Gen. C. C. Augur, when Edwin M. Stanton, Secretary of War, sent the following telegram to New York City:

"Washington, April 16th, 1865.
"3:20 P. M.

"Col. L. C. Baker—Come here immediately and see if you can find the murderer of the President.

"(Signed.)   EDWIN M. STANTON,
"Secretary of War."

Early the next morning Col. Baker reached Washington, accompanied by his cousin, Lieut. L. B. Baker, a member of the Bureau, who had recently been mustered out of the First District of Columbia Cavalry.

They went at once to the office of the War Department and after a conference with Secretary Stanton, began the search for the murderer of the President.

"Up to this time," says Col. Baker, "the confusion had been so great that few of the ordinary detective measures for the apprehension of criminals had been employed. No rewards had been offered. Little or no attempt had been made to collect and arrange the clue in the furtherance of a systematic search and the pursuit was wholly without a dictating leadership."

Col. Baker's first step was the publication of a handbill offering thirty thousand dollars for the capture of the fugitives. Twenty thousand dollars of this amount was subscribed by the City of Washington and the other ten thousand dollars by Col. Baker, offered on his own account and authorized by the War Department.

On this handbill was a minute description of Booth, as follows:

"John Wilkes Booth, who assassinated the President on the evening of April 14th, 1865, height 5 feet 8 inches, weight 160 pounds, compactly built; hair jet black, inclined to curl; medium length, parted behind, eyes black, and heavy brows. Wears a large seal ring on his little finger.

"When talking inclines his head forward and looks down.

"(Signed.)   L. C. BAKER,
    "Colonel and Adjutant of the War Dept."

Hardly had these handbills been posted when the United States Government made the publication of additional reward to the amount of one hundred thousand dollars for the capture of Booth, Surratt and Herold, Surratt at that time being suspected of dire complicity in the assassination.

Three states increased this sum by twenty-five thousand dollars each and many individuals and companies, shocked by the awful atrocity of the crime, offered rewards of various amounts. Fabulous stories were told of the wealth which the assassin's captors would receive, the sum being placed anywhere from five hundred thousand dollars to one million dollars.

This prospect of winning a fortune at once set hundreds of detectives and recently discharged Union officers and soldiers, and, in fact, a vast host of adventurers into the field of search and the whole of Southern Maryland and Eastern Virginia was scoured and ransacked until it seemed as if a jack rabbit could not have escaped, and yet at the end of ten days the assassins were still at large.

"Booth was accompanied in his flight by a callow stage-struck youth named David E. Herold, who was bound to Booth, the older, merely by ties of a marvelous magnetism as a part of his art."

134

THE HAND OF SECRETARY STANTON.

"In beginning his search for the assassin Col. Baker proceeded on the theory that Jefferson Davis, President of the Confederate States, and his Cabinet, were involved in the plot and that Booth, Herold and others, were mere tools in the hands of the more skilled conspirators. He therefore detailed Lieut. L. B. Baker to procure for the purpose of future identification, photographs of John Wilkes Booth, Jefferson Davis, President of the Confederacy; George N. Sanders, Beverly Tucker, Jacob Thompson and others unknown, all of whom were charged with being conspirators.

"Lieutenant Baker, with half a dozen active men to help him, was sent into lower Maryland to distribute the handbills describing Booth, Herold and others, and to exhibit the pictures of the fugitives when possible, under instructions from Col. Baker. They also made a search for clues, but they found themselves harassed and thwarted at Washington by private detectives and soldiers who tried to throw them off their trail (as Baker thought), in the hope of following it successfully themselves."

In this connection I challenge attention to the conduct of Gen. Dana, as we left him at Bryantown resting under the seeming shadows of treacherous conduct, which accusation appears also to be well founded by the statements of Col. Baker, for he says that in their search for Booth and Herold they found themselves harassed and thwarted at every turn by private detectives and soldiers of the Federal Army who tried to throw them off the trail.

Baker says they regarded Booth, Herold and others as "mere tools in the hands of more skilled conspirators." Baker was more wise than even he knew in this conclusion as the events of after years disclosed, proven by the confession of Booth himself of the plot and the persons connected with it.

"On his return to Washington Lieut. Baker told Col. Baker that it was his opinion that Booth and his companions had not gone South, but had taken some other direction, most probably toward Philadelphia, where it was known that Booth had several women friends.

" 'Now, sir,' was Col. Baker's answer, 'you are mistaken. There is no place of safety for them on earth, except among their friends in the still rebellious South.'

"Acting on this belief, Col. Baker, Theodore Woodall, one of the detectives in lower Maryland, accompanied by an expert telegrapher named Brakwith, who was to attach his instrument to the wires at any convenient point and report frequently to headquarters at Washington, started in pursuit of Booth.

"These men had been out less than two days when they discovered a valuable clue from a negro who told them without hesitation that two men answering the description of Booth and Herold had crossed the Potomac below Port Tobacco on Sunday night, April 21st, 1865, in a fishing boat.

"This evidence or information was regarded as of so much importance that the negro was hurried to Washington by the next boat on the Potomac river. Col. Baker questioned him closely and after showing him a large number of photographs he at once selected the picture of Booth and Herold as being the persons whom he had seen in the boat. Col. Baker decided that the clue was of the first importance and, after a hurried conference with Secretary Stanton, he sent a request to Gen. Hancock for a detachment of cavalry to guard his men sent in pursuit and Lieut. Baker was ordered to the quartermaster's department to make arrangements for transportation down the Potomac river. On Lieut. Baker's return he was informed that he and E. J. Conger and other detectives were to have charge of the party.

"The three men then held a conference in which Col. Baker fully explained his theory of the whereabouts of Booth and Herold. In half an hour Lieut. Edward P. Dougherty, of the 16th New York Cavalry, with twenty-five men, Sergeant Boston Corbett, second in command, reported to Col. Baker for duty, having been directed to go with Lieut. Baker and Conger wherever they might order and to protect them to the extent of their ability. Without waiting even to secure sufficient rations Lieut. Baker and his men galloped off down to the Sixth Street dock and hurried on the government tug, 'John S. Ide,' at a little after three o'clock, and that same afternoon the tug reached Belle Plain Landing. At this point there was a sharp bend in the river and Col. Baker advised his men to scour the strip of country stretching between it and the Rappahannock river.

"On disembarking Baker and Conger rode continuously ahead, Lieut. Dougherty and his men following within hailing distance. The country being familiar to both of the leaders of the expedition they assumed the names of well-known blockade runners and mail carriers and stopped at the homes of the more prominent Confederates to make inquiries, saying:

" 'We are being pursued by the Yankees and in crossing the river we became separated from two of our party, one of whom is a lame man. Have you seen them?'

"All night this kind of work was kept up, interspersed with much harder riding, but although the Confederates invariably expressed their sympathy it was evident that they knew nothing of the fugitives. At dawn the cavalrymen threw off their disguise and halted for an hour for rest and refreshments.

"Again in their saddles they struck across the country in the direction of Port Conway, a little town on the Rappahannock river, about twenty-two miles below Fredericksburg. Between two and three o'clock in the afternoon they drew rein near a planter's home, half a mile distant from this town, and ordered dinner for the men and feed for their horses. Conger, who was suffering from an old wound, was almost exhausted from the long, hot and dusty ride. He and the other members of the party, except Baker and a corporal, dropped down on the roadside to rest. Baker, fearing that the presence of the scouting party might give warning to Booth and his companions, should they be hiding in the neighborhood, pushed on ahead to the bank of the Rappahannock river. He saw dozing in the sunshine in front of his little cottage a fisherman, or ferryman, whose name was Rollins. He asked him if he had seen a lame man cross the river within the past few days. The man answered yes he had, and that there were other men with him. In fact he had ferried them across the river.. (This was Booth, Herold and Ruddy. Notice that the ferryman refers to men being with Booth—not a man).

"Baker drew out his photographs and without hesitation Rollins pointed out the pictures of Booth and Herold. (Baker had no picture of Ruddy).

" 'These men,' he said, nodding his head, 'They are the men, only this one,' pointing to Booth's picture, 'had no mustache.' (The fisherman evidently was thinking of Ruddy and identifying him from Booth's picture, because Booth had a mustache and Ruddy did not have a distinguishable mustache, having an even growth of whiskers on his entire face. This would seem to show that Ruddy could have been, and was, mistaken for Booth, without a long mustache.)

"It was with a thrill of satisfaction that Baker heard these words. He was now positive that he of all the hundred detectives and soldiers who were looking for Booth, was on the right trail. Not a moment was to be lost now that the object of their search might be riding far into the land of the Rebels. Baker sent the corporal back with orders for Conger and his men to come up without delay. After he was gone Rollins explained that the men had hired him to ferry them across the river on the previous afternoon and that just before starting three men had ridden up and greeted the fugitives.

"In response to questioning Rollins admitted that he knew the three men well; that they were Major M. B. Ruggles, Lieut. Bainbridge and Capt. Jett, of Mosby's Confederate command.

" ' Do you know where they went?' Baker pressed the questioning.

" 'Wall,' drawled the fisherman, 'this Capt. Jett has a lady love over at Bowling Green and I reckon he went over there.' And he further explained that Bowling Green was about fifteen miles to the south and that it had a big hotel which would make a good hiding place for a wounded man. As the cavalry came up Baker told Rollins that he would have to accompany him as a guide until they reached Bowling Green. To this Rollins objected on the ground that he would incur the hatred of his neighbors, none of whom had favored the Union cause.

" 'But you might make me your prisoner,' he said in his slow drawl, 'then I would have to go.' Baker felt the necessity of exercising the greatest energy in the pursuit if the fugitives were to be snatched from the shelter of the hostile country.

"Rollins' old ferry boat was shaky and, although the loading was done with the greatest dispatch it took three trips to get the detachment across the river, when the march for Bowling Green was begun. The horses sweltered up the crooked sandy road from the river. Baker and Conger, who were riding ahead, saw two horsemen standing motionless on the top of a hill, their black forms showing well against the sky. (This was Major or Lieut. Ruggles and Bainbridge on sentinel duty, guarding Booth at the Garrett farm, which was only a short distance to the north of where these men were seen).

"These men seem much interested in the movements of the cavalry. Baker and Conger at once suspected them of being Booth's friends, who had in some way received information of the approach of the searching party.

"Baker signaled the horsemen to wait for a parley but instead of stopping they at once put spurs to their horses and galloped up the road. Conger and Baker gave chase, but they bent to the necks of their horses and riding at full speed they were away. And just as they were overhauling them the two horsemen dashed into a blind trail leading from the main road into the pine forest. (This is when Ruggles and Bainbridge rode to the Garrett home, a short distance north of the main road, in which the Federal troops then were on their way to Bowling Green, and then it was that they notified Booth to leave the Garrett home, as explained to me by St.

142

Helen (or Booth), when he left the Garrett home and went into the wooded spot where he was afterward picked up by Ruggles and Bainbridge, and furnished a horse by which means he made his escape.)

"The pursuers drew rein on their winded horses and after consultation decided not to follow further, but to reach Bowling Green as promptly as possible." These men, Baker and Conger say, they were afterward informed, were Ruggles and Bainbridge, and that Booth, at the time they turned back, was less than half a mile away, lying on the grass in front of the Garrett house. Baker says further that "indeed Booth saw his pursuers distinctly as they neared his hiding place and commented on their dusty and saddle-worn appearance." (In this Baker is mistaken. Booth did not see them, but was informed of their movements only by Ruggles and Bainbridge.)

Baker and Conger believed Booth to be at Bowling Green, fifteen miles away, and so they pushed on, leaving behind the man they so much desired to capture.

"It was near midnight when the party clattered into Bowling Green, and with hardly a spoken command surrounded the dark, rambling hotel. Baker stepped boldly to the front door, while Conger strode to the rear from which came the dismal barking of a dog. Presently a light flickered on and some one opened the door ajar and inquired in a frightened, feminine voice, what was wanted. Baker thrust his toe inside, flung the door open and was confronted by a woman. At this moment Conger came through from the back way, led by a negro. The woman admitted at once that there was a Confederate cavalryman sleeping in the house and promptly pointed out the room. Baker and Conger, candle in hand, at once entered. Capt. Jett sat up staring at them and said:

" 'What do you want?'

" 'We want you,' answered Conger. 'You took Booth across the river, and you know where he is.'

" 'You are mistaken in your man,' Jett replied rolling out of bed.

" 'You lie!' roared Conger, springing forward, his pistol close to Jett's head.

"By this time the cavalrymen had crowded into the room and Jett saw the candle light glinting on their brass buttons and on their drawn revolvers.

" 'Upon my honor as a gentleman,' he said, paling, 'I will tell you all I know if you will shield me from complicity in the whole matter.'

" 'Yes, if we get Booth,' responded Conger.

" 'Booth is at the Garrett home, three miles this side of Port Conway,' he said. 'If you came that way you may have frightened him off, for you must have passed the place.

"In less than thirty minutes the pursuing party was doubling back over the road by which it had just come, bearing Jett with it as a prisoner.

"The bridle reins of the horse ridden by him were fastened to the men on each side of him in the fear that he would make a dash to escape and alarm Booth and Herold.

"It was a black night, no moon, no stars, and the dust rose in choking clouds. For two days the men had eaten little and slept less, and they were so worn out that they could hardly sit on their jaded horses, and yet they plunged and stumbled on through the darkness over fifteen miles of meandering country road, reaching the Garrett home at half-past 3 or 4 o'clock on the morning of April 26, 1865.

"Like many other Southern places, Garrett's home stood far back from the road, with a bridle gate at the end of a long lane. So exhausted were the cavalrymen that some of them dropped down in the sand when their horses stopped and had to be kicked into wakefulness. Rollins and Jett were placed under guard and Baker and Conger made a dash up the lane, some of the cavalry following. Garrett's house was an old-fashioned southern mansion, somewhat dilapidated, with a wide hospitable piazza, reaching its full length in front, and barns and tobacco houses looming up big and dark apart.

"Baker leaped from his horse to the steps and thundered on the door. A moment later a window close at hand was cautiously raised and a man thrust his head out. Before he could say a word Baker seized him by the arm and said: 'Open the door! Be quick about it!' The old man, trembling, complied, and Baker stepped inside, closing the door behind him. A candle was quickly lighted, and then Baker demanded of Garrett to reveal the hiding place of the men who had been staying in the house.

" 'They are gone to the woods,' he said. (This was true, as Booth had gone to the woods about 2 or 3 o'clock the day before, when notified by Ruggles and Bainbridge.) Baker thrust his revolver in the old man's face: 'Don't tell me that,' he said. 'They are here.'

"Conger now came in with young Garrett. 'Don't injure father,' said the young man. 'I will tell you all about it. The men did go to the woods last evening when some cavalry went by, but came back and wanted us to take them over to Louisa Court House.' (Booth had left as the old man Garrett said.)

146

"The men spoken of by young Garrett as coming back were Herold and Ruddy, returning from Bowling Green, as prearranged at the Rappahannock Ferry, and explained to me by St. Helen (Booth) to meet Booth, who they found had gone. They remained that night with the Garretts. There was no one with Booth at the Garrett's, and when he left he left alone. Ruggles and Bainbridge corroborate St. Helen (Booth), and say that when they returned to the Garrett home and notified Booth to leave they looked for Herold, who had not yet returned to Booth, and that Booth straightway left by himself, in the direction which they pointed out to him. So the allusion by young Garrett to the two men returning had no reference to Booth's return, for at the time Booth left the Garrett home Herold and Ruddy had not yet reached there on their return from Bowling Green.

"Young Garrett, continuing, said to Baker: 'We could not leave home before morning, if at all. We were becoming suspicious of them and father told them they could not stay with us.'

" 'Where are they now?' interrupted Baker.

" 'In the barn. My brother locked them in for fear they would steal the horses. He is now keeping watch on them in the corn crib.'

"It was plain that Garrett did not know the identity of the men who had been imposing on their hospitality. Baker asked no questions, but taking young Garrett's arm he made a dash toward the barn, when Conger ordered the cavalrymen to follow, and formed them in such position around the barn that no one could escape. By this time the soldiers had found the boy guarding the barn and had brought him out with the key. Baker unlocked the door and told young Garrett that inasmuch as the two men were his guests he must go inside and induce them to come out and surrender. The young man objected most vigorously.

" 'They are armed to the teeth,' he faltered, 'and they will shoot me down.' But he appreciated the fact that he was looking into the black mouth of Baker's revolver and hastily slid through the doorway.

"There was a sudden rustling of corn blades and the sound of voices in low conversation. All around the barn the soldiers were picketed, wrapped in inky blackness and uttering no sound. In the midst of a little circle of candle light Baker stood at the doorway with drawn revolver. Conger had gone to the rear of the barn.

"During the heat and excitement of the chase Baker had assumed command of the cavalrymen,

148

somewhat to the umbrage of Lieut. Dougherty, who kept himself in the background during the remainder of the night. Further away, around the house, the Garrett family huddled together trembling and frightened.

"Suddenly from the barn a clear, high voice rang out, 'You have betrayed me, sir! Leave this barn or I will shoot you!'

"Baker then called to the men in the barn, ordering them to turn over their arms to young Garrett and surrender at once. 'If you don't, we shall burn the barn, and have a bonfire and a shooting match.' At this young Garrett came running to the door and begged to be let out. He said he would do anything he could, but he did not want to risk his life in the presence of the two desperate men.

"Baker then opened the door and Garrett came out with a bound. He turned and pointed to the candle which Baker had been carrying since he left the house. 'Put that out, or he will· shoot you by its light,' he whispered in a frightened voice. Baker placed the candle on the ground at a little distance from the door, so that it would light all the space in front of the barn. Then he called to Booth to surrender. In a full, clear voice Booth replied:

" 'There is a man here who wishes to surrender.' And they heard him say to Herold: 'Leave me, will you? Go! I don't want you to stay!'

"At the door Herold was whimpering, 'Let me out! Let me out! I know nothing of this man in here.' (As a matter of fact Herold knew nothing of the man in there with him, who was Ruddy, with whom he had been connected only as the employe and guide for Booth, from across the Potomac and Rappahannock rivers, and with whom Herold had gone to Bowling Green and returned to the Garrett home, as explained by Booth to me.)

" 'Bring out your arms and you can surrender,' insisted Baker.

"Herold did not have any arms, and Booth (as they called him), finally said: 'He has no arms. The arms are mine, and I shall keep them.' By this time Herold was praying pieteously to be let out. He said he was afraid of being shot, and begged to be allowed to surrender.

"Baker opened the door a little and told him to put out his hands. The moment the door opened Baker seized his hands and whipped Herold out of the barn and turned him over to the soldiers.

" 'You had better come out, too,' said Baker to Booth (or the man in the barn.)

" 'Tell me who you are and what you want of me. It may be that I am being taken by my friends.'

" 'It makes no difference who we are,' was the reply. 'We know you and we want you. We have fifty well armed men stationed around this barn. You cannot escape, and we do not wish to kill you.'

"There was a moment's pause and then Booth (as they supposed), said, falteringly: 'Captain, that is a hard case. I swear I am lame. Give me a chance. Draw up your men twenty yards from here, and I will fight your whole command.'

" 'We are not here to fight,' said Baker. 'We are here to take you.'

"Booth (as they supposed him) then asked for time to consider, and Baker told him that he could have two minutes—no more. Presently he said: 'Captain, I believe you are a brave and honorable man. I have had half a dozen chances to shoot you. I have had a bead drawn on you, and I have a bead drawn on you now. I do not wish to kill you. Withdraw your men from the door and I will go out. Give me this chance for my life. I will not be taken alive.'

"Even in his deep distress Booth had not forgotten to be theatrical.

" 'Your time is up,' said Baker, firmly. 'If you don't come out we shall fire the barn.'

" 'Well, then, my brave boys,' came the answer in clarion tones, which could be heard by the women who cowered on the Garrett porch rods away, 'you may prepare a stretcher for me.'

"Then after a slight pause he added, 'One more star on the glorious old banner.'

"Conger now came .around the corner of the barn and asked Baker if he was ready. Baker nodded and Conger stepped noiselessly back, drew a husk of corn blades through the crack in the barn, scratched a match, and in a moment the whole interior of the barn was brilliant with light. Baker opened the door and peered in. Booth (as they supposed) had been lying against the mow, but he now sprang forward, half blinded by the glow of the fire, his crutches under his arms and his carbine leveled in the direction of the flames as if he would shoot the man who had set them going, but he could not see in the darkness outside. He hesitated, then reeled forward again. An old table was near at hand. He caught hold of it as though to cast it top side down on the fire, but he was not quick enough, and dropping one crutch he hobbled toward the door. About the middle of the barn he stopped, drew himself up to his full height and seemed to take in the entire situation. His hat was gone, and his waving, dark hair was tossed back from his high, white forehead, his lips were firmly compressed, and if he was pale the ruddy glow of the firelight concealed the fact.

"In his full, dark eyes there was an expression of mingled hatred and terror, and the defiance of a tiger hunted to his lair. In one hand he held a carbine, in the other a revolver, and his belt contained another revolver and a bowie knife. He seemed prepared to fight to the end, no matter what numbers appeared against him. By this time the flames in the dry corn blades had mounted to the rafters of the dingy old building, arching the hunted assassin in a glow of fire more brilliant than the lightnings of any theater in which he had ever played.

"Suddenly Booth (as they supposed him) threw aside his remaining crutch, dropped his carbine, raised his revolver and made a spring for the door. It was his evident intention to shoot down any one who might bar his way, and make a dash for liberty, fighting as he ran.

"Then came a shock that sounded above the roar of the flames. Booth (as they supposed him) leaped in the air, then pitched forward on his face. Baker was on him in an instant and grasped both his arms to prevent the use of the revolver, but this precaution was entirely unnecessary. Booth (as they supposed him) would struggle no more. Another moment and Conger and the soldiers came rushing in while Baker turned the wounded man over and felt for his heart.

" 'He must have shot himself,' remarked Baker. 'I saw him the moment the fire was lighted. If not, the man who did do the shooting goes back to Washington in irons for disobedience of orders.'

"In the excitement that followed the firing of the barn Sergeant Corbett, an eccentric character who had accompanied the cavalry detachment, had stepped up to the side of the barn, placed his revolver to a crack between two boards, and just as Booth (as they supposed him) was about to spring to the doorway he had fired the fatal shot.

"Booth's (as they supposed it) body was caught up and carried out of the barn and laid under an apple tree not far away. Water was dashed in his face and Baker tried to make him drink, but he seemed unable to swallow. Presently, however, he opened his eyes and seemed to understand the situation. His lips moved, and Baker bent down to hear what he might say. 'Tell mother—— Tell mother ——' he faltered, and then became unconscious.

"The flames of the burning barn now grew so intense that it was necessary to remove the dying man to the piazza of the house, where he was laid on a mattress provided by Mrs. Garrett. A cloth wet with brandy was applied to his lips, and under this influence he revived a little, then opened his

154

eyes and said with deep bitterness: 'Oh, kill me. Kill me quick!'

" 'No, Booth,' (they supposed him Booth), 'we don't want you to die. You were shot against orders.'

"Then he was unconscious again for several minutes and they thought he would never speak again, but his breast heaved and he acted as if he wished to say something.

"Baker placed his ear at the dying man's mouth and Booth (so they supposed) faltered: 'Tell mother I died for my country. I did what I thought was best.' With a feeling of pity and tenderness Baker lifted the limp hand, but it fell back again by his side as if dead. Booth (as they supposed) seemed conscious of the movement. He turned his eyes and muttered 'Hopeless, useless,' and he was dead."

I must be pardoned for cutting short the circuitous and superfluous language Baker employs in his further narrative on reaching Washington with the body of the man he supposed to be Booth, but will condense his statements. He says the body was taken from the Garrett home to the river and placed on the gunboat from which they had disembarked (the steamer John S. Ide), and thence up the Potomac river to Washington City, where the body was removed to another gunboat, Sangatuck, lying at anchor near the navy yard. An autopsy and inquest was held here, the bullet was taken out of the head of the body and produced as evidence of the cause of the death of the man whose body they had. Then Conger produced such evidence as they had of the identity of the body as that of John Wilkes Booth, which follows: The diary, the letters or papers and the pictures of Booth's two relatives, the carbines, the belt and a compass, which were placed in the hands of Col. Baker, in charge of the body, and all of which Col. Baker delivered to the officers of the Secretary of War, and the body, without further identification, was buried in a cell on the ground floor of the old navy prison.

So much for the article of Mr. Ray Stannard Baker, a relative of Col. L. C. Baker, and Lieut. L. B. Baker, as refers to the pursuit of and supposed capture and killing of John Wilkes Booth, which is reproduced above because he writes of the subject as of information from Lieut. L. B. Baker, the man who was last in pursuit of Booth, and who is supposed to have captured and killed Booth.

By a casual reading, and without investigation, the statements made by Mr. Ray Stannard Baker would seem conclusive, but it will be seen that Mr. Baker has stated fiction for facts, assuming without proof that the man in the supposed barn or crib was Booth, and that the man killed was Booth, the truth of which fact must rest on the subsequent identification of the body which Lieut. Baker carried to Washington, assuming it to be the body of Booth. Upon this proof of identification of the body by Conger, who produced Booth's two pictures and the papers mentioned, together with a carbine, a belt and a compass, they were placed in the hands of Col. Baker and were the only proof offered for the identification of Booth.

Does this prove the body to be that of Booth? No, not directly, not positively. But the evidence offered was merely circumstantial, if found on the body of the dead man, as tending to show that it was the body of Booth, upon the presumption that such things as belonged to Booth would be found on his body, but does not negative the probability or possibility of finding these matters of evidence on the body of some man other than Booth. It is claimed, and history discloses, that none of the pursuing party under Lieut. Baker, nor even he himself, knew either Booth or Herold, but they were furnished photographs of them for their identification, while at the inquest the body was not identified by the picture of Booth, so far as we are informed, though it was then and there in the possession of Lieut.

Baker. There was no further proof of the identity of the body as that of Booth except the pictures of Booth's relatives, the letters, etc., offered by Conger, and this was solely relied on. If the body had been that of Booth positive identification could have been had by comparison with his pictures, while hundreds, yea, perhaps thousands of the people living in Washington could have been called on to positively identify the dead body of Booth under oath. There were so many who knew him personally and others who had so often seen him on the stage that it would have been almost as easy to have identified the body of John Wilkes Booth as that of President Lincoln, whom he had assassinated. Why was not this done? Because even Lieut. Baker says: "Indeed, there were rumors widely circulated in certain parts of the country that Booth had never been captured." And before the trial of the conspirators was begun he was again sent into lower Maryland to collect evidence against Booth and his accomplices, and was so far successful as to find the boat in which Booth and Herold had crossed the Potomac river, and Booth's opera glasses hidden near the Garrett home, both of which he took back to Washington.

How is it that Baker, on his second visit, found Booth's opera, or field glasses, hidden near the Garrett home? It is evidence of two things: First, that Booth had been out from the Garrett home, as he was when notified by Ruggles and Bainbridge to go to the wooded spot near the Garrett house and wait for them, where they would come for him (which Booth said he did), and this is how and why the glasses were found, as Baker says, "hidden near the Garrett home," lost or dropped by Booth as he sought the secluded hiding place in the woods.

Second, it was not Booth in the barn, as they supposed. If it had been they would have found the glasses there, as we have no record of Booth having left the Garrett home, except by Booth (St. Helen), and by Ruggles and Bainbridge, who say that Booth was alone when they notified him to leave. They looked for Herold and he was not there. This was a fact, for Herold had not returned with Ruddy from Bowling Green, and they did not reach the Garrett home until 10 o'clock on the night of the day that Booth left the Garrett home (at about 2 or 3 o'clock in the afternoon). Of this we have the preponderance of proof, to-wit: Ruggles and Bainbridge say they "found Booth on the lawn in front of the Garrett home and notified him to leave;" that he did leave alone, and that they especially looked for Herold and he was not present.

St. Helen, or Booth, says he left the Garrett home alone. Old man Garrett said, in reply to Lieut. Baker, that they had gone to the woods, referring to Booth, Ruggles and Bainbridge, while young Garrett said to Lieut. Baker they had returned, referring to Ruddy and Herold, who had come in late that evening from Bowling Green, Virginia, expecting to meet Booth, where Booth had agreed to remain in waiting for them, and would have done so, except for the warning from Ruggles and Bainbridge five or six hours before Herold and Ruddy returned.

It is evident that the government was not satisfied with the only proof they had of Booth's death, to-wit: The letters, pictures, etc., furnished them by Conger and Baker, that the body turned over to it by Baker and Conger was actually that of Booth; and were much puzzled by the circumstances of finding Booth's letters, etc., on this body which was claimed to be that of Booth, and this was at least a strong circumstantial evidence of identity to those who did not know Booth by sight; but in Washington City there was no excuse for not obtaining positive identification of Booth's body because there were hundreds of people there who knew him personally.

If the government had been satisfied that the body delivered by Baker and Conger was that of John Wilkes Booth I dare say it would have been placed on public exhibition rather than have been held in the secret manner in which it was. At least, the body would have been sufficiently exposed for public and positive identification, which would have been a matter of general satisfaction to the American people, for all sections of the country were clamoring for the execution of the man who had taken the life of President Lincoln. For some reason this was not done, and it has not been done to this day, as will be learned upon the further reading of this story, where, in an unofficial statement from the War Department, it is admitted that the government has no direct or positive evidence of the capture and death of John Wilkes Booth. In fact, the government has no proof of the capture and death of John Wilkes Booth other than the finding of the letters, pictures, etc., of Booth on the body of the man captured, killed and delivered by Baker and Conger.

Again, observe the minuteness and apparent perfection of detail of Mr. Ray Stannard Baker, who was not present, but who assumes to speak as one present, presenting the most minute act, movement, to the very utterances and tone of voice attributed to Booth, in the supposed burning of the barn or corn crib, and that, too, written thirty-two years after the supposed capture and killing took place.

That is, Booth was supposed to have been killed on or about April 26, 1865, and Mr. Baker writes and publishes his article in May, 1897, and admits that he was not present at the time in the pursuit of Booth, and personally knew nothing of what he wrote. Therefore, the physical facts and admissions condemn Mr. Baker's article as one of misinformation and pure invention or fiction—a misleading statement of an historical occurrence. For instance, he refers to the dark outlines of the dingy barn and tobacco house, where Booth is claimed to have been killed, when, as a matter of fact, was there a barn on the place at all, or only two small corn cribs constructed of poles or small logs, as is seen in the true pictures of the Garrett home here presented? Boston Corbett, himself, recently said that he "shot Booth in a little house through a crack." Boston Corbett was present and shot the man who was killed, so it will be seen that Baker's description of the barn is purely one of his imagination.

Again, Baker has this man, supposed to be Booth, on two crutches in the barn, within the glare of the burning barn, when, as a matter of fact, Booth at no time had two crutches, but used only one, that made from an old broom handle by Dr. Mudd ten days prior to the time of which Baker writes, and this

DAVID E. HEROLD.

The Accomplice of John Wilkes Booth, and the Garrett
Home, Where He Was Captured, Ruddy Killed, and From
Which Booth Escaped, Going to the Wooded Spot Just
North of the House.

BRYANTOWN,

The Place Gen. Dana Reached on the Morning and Remained
During the Day of April 15th, 1865, While Booth Was
Resting That Same Day at the Home of Dr. Mudd, Only
Three and a Half Miles Away.

was discarded by Booth before he reached the Garrett home. At the Garrett home Booth was merely using a stick for support, the injury to his leg being a sprained ankle and slight fracture of the shin bone, about six inches above the ankle, and when Booth left the Garrett's he was only using this stick. Again, if there was no barn to burn—and we understand there was none—then none was burned, as claimed and written of by Mr. Baker. The man killed was killed in the left hand corn crib, as you face them in the picture of the Garrett home and barnyard, shown in this volume, which is a true reproduction of the Garrett home, together with the corn cribs as they were on the 26th day of April, 1865, and as we presume they are now. So that Baker neither had Booth, a barn or even a large corn crib for the tragic play he writes of Booth and his killing at the Garrett home on the early morning of the 26th day of April, 1865. So his sentimental and pathetic story of the capture and killing of Booth is one drawn from his imagination, written principally, it would appear, for the purpose of robbing Lieutenant E. P. Dougherty of his share in the participation of the famous pursuit and supposed capture of Booth, who, as a matter of fact, had command of the squad of cavalry in pursuit of Booth, and is justly entitled to any credit that is due the commander of this now famous troop; for it was Dougherty who was the superior officer in command of the whole campaign in pursuit of Booth, under the direction of Col. L. C. Baker, who remained at Washington. As a matter of fact, Mr. Baker's article is an apparent plagiarism of Capt. Edward P. Dougherty's report of his pursuit, capture and killing of the man supposed to be John Wilkes Booth, published in January, 1890, twenty-five years after the incident; while Mr. Baker writes and publishes his remarkable story seven years after Capt. Dougherty's is published and thirty-two years after the supposed killing of Booth.

Before leaving the subject of the personages found at the Garrett home and the facts reported by the Federal troops in command of Capt. Dougherty, we wish to say that from all obtainable proof on both sides, which best harmonizes with reason and is most consonant with truth, Booth was carried to the Garrett home by Ruggles and Bainbridge, who remained to watch over him until Herold and Ruddy should return from Bowling Green. And before Herold and Ruddy could return for Booth, as had been prearranged the day before the troops came in pursuit, they having to walk going and coming from the Garrett home to Bowling Green, a distance of twenty to twenty-four miles, the nearest route they could travel from Ports Royal and Conway would require the entire afternoon of the day they crossed the Rappahannock river, or more, to reach Bowling Green, and they most likely remained there half of the forenoon of the next day, so they could not have reached the Garrett home before late in the evening if they left Bowling Green at 12 o'clock noon. And there is some proof to show they did arrive at the Garrett home about 10 o'clock that night—the same day on which Booth left the Garrett home in the afternoon—and that as a fact Ruddy and Herold were at the Garrett home asleep in the back or shed room of the house, which has a door opening out in direct line to the gate opening into the horse lot, as they are commonly called in the upland countries of the South. Booth left the Garrett home about 2 or 3 o'clock in the afternoon and Ruddy and Herold arrived at the Garrett home about 10 o'clock that night, six or seven hours later. Thus when Capt. Dougherty, guided by Jett, came upon the Garrett home and surrounded the house on the early morning of the next day—the morning following the day on which Booth left—they found Ruddy and Herold asleep in this back room, who, when awakened by hearing the noise made by the Federal troops around the house, with Capt Dougherty demanding admission from old man Garrett at the front entrance of the house, made a dash under cover of the darkness (the hour being between 3 and 4 o'clock in the morning) for the first hiding place, making their escape out of this back doorway through the gate mentioned and went into the corn crib, where they were discovered. They were located in this crib and surrounded by the soldiers, and Herold was taken a prisoner. And it was here in this crib that Boston Corbett, against orders, shot and killed the man supposed to be John Wilkes Booth. The body of Ruddy was taken from the crib, after being shot, and on his body was found the letters, etc., belonging to Booth which Ruddy had taken from the wagon after Booth had left the ferry and which he was trying to deliver to Booth at the Garrett home, as promised at their last meeting, but which, because Booth was gone, he could not deliver. So when Ruddy was killed they were found on his body. Finding the letters, pictures, etc., belonging to Booth on the body of the man who was killed, Capt. Dougherty reached the conclusion that the body in his possession was that of John Wilkes Booth, and thus it was that through the circumstances mentioned the body of Ruddy was identified as the body of John Wilkes Booth.

Two facts we wish to emphasize—they are unanswerable—brought out and agreed upon by all that has been written and said on the subject. They are: First, that Booth was carried to the Garrett home by Ruggles and Bainbridge, Confederate soldiers belonging to Mosby's command. Second, that Booth had notice of the pursuit by the Federal troops; that being notified by Ruggles and Bainbridge, Booth did leave the Garrett home at their urgent request for his (Booth's) safety; that they did see him leave alone, with the earnest and determined purpose to make good his escape, with a full knowledge of his present and impending danger of being captured, which he knew was death.

Can any one, under these circumstances and conditions, believe that Booth did not go and continue to go? Can any one believe that he would at that time have returned to the Garrett home? The sane and reasonable answer to these queries is unquestionably and unequivocally—NO.

CHAPTER XII.

GEN. DANA IDENTIFIES BOOTH.

After having read the publication of Gen. Dana in December, 1897, I remembered anew the incidents connected with the confessions of St. Helen and went persistently to work to ascertain, if possible, the truth with respect to the escape of John Wilkes Booth.

I wrote at once to Gen. Dana for further facts.

Having no knowledge whatever of the Booth family before my meeting with St. Helen, I could only explain the information I had received from him concerning this family and the escape of John Wilkes Booth upon the theory that St. Helen was related to Herold and knew Booth's personal and family affairs by reason of his association with either Booth or Herold, or both. So, I assumed, without foundation in fact, that the tintype picture of himself given me by St. Helen when he believed he was dying must be a picture of some one of the Herolds. So I wrote Gen. Dana, who in return sent me the first pictures I ever remember to have

168

seen of Booth, also Herold and others. I at once identified John Wilkes Booth for the first time, by comparing the tintype picture of St. Helen with the picture of John Wilkes Booth sent me by Dana. St. Helen was indeed the man he claimed to be—John Wilkes Booth. I at once had a picture made from the tintype and sent it to Dana, whose reply, from Lubec, Maine, January 17, 1898, with respect to this picture, is as follows:

"Dear Sir: Your favor of January 8th at hand and read. I must say I was somewhat surprised at the turn things took, for I expected the likeness of Herold, or that it would have some of the features in it of the man Herold you wrote me about, but it seems it was Booth instead.

"Can this be J. B. Booth, brother of John Wilkes Booth? Will it be asking too much of you to send me a copy of the confession which you have? I would like to have it for my own satisfaction. If I can be of any help to you, will gladly aid all I can. Regarding J. B. Booth, I shall write to some one of the Booth family and learn all I can of his death, and where. When received will send to you.

"Respectfully yours, etc.,

"(Signed.)   DAVID D. DANA."

GEN. DANA IDENTIFIES BOOTH.

Especial attention is called to Gen. Dana's identification of the tintype picture as that of John Wilkes Booth, and his intimate knowledge of the Booth family, asking as he does if this picture is that of his brother, J. B. Booth, and the readiness with which he could approach "some one of the Booth family and learn all I can of his death," getting all the information he desired of J. B. Booth, whom he claimed to be dead, and whose name had in no way been brought into the discussion except by Gen. Dana. But for some reason unknown to me Gen. Dana did not write giving me the information which he had voluntarily promised.

Why?

I have since learned, however, that the brother of Booth unmistakably referred to by Gen. Dana as J. B. Booth was Junius Brutus Booth, the oldest brother of John Wilkes Booth, who, with the exception of a few years spent in the West, lived and died in Boston, Mass. The next eldest brother lived and died in New York City. The youngest brother, Dr. Joseph Adrian Booth, a physician of acknowledged ability, was associated with his brother, Edwin Booth, the famous actor of New York City, in a business way other than that of acting, as he made no pretention to the stage, died some years ago, I am informed.

Of these four brothers only John Wilkes Booth came South, and he only after the assassination of President Lincoln, the other brothers living and dying in the East.

The entire Booth family, consisting of two sisters and four brothers, of which John Wilkes was one, were similar in appearance, and you would recognize a family likeness, yet they were very unlike in many features, so that no one knowing the family could mistake one for the other. This statement is made from actual knowledge, for I have before me the pictures of the entire Booth family, the father and mother, four brothers and two sisters, which constitutes the entire family. Should any one doubt the accuracy of this statement or be curious to see, he may dispel the one and gratify the other by securing a copy of the Cincinnati Enquirer, published April 27, 1902, and find the group referred to at page 1, section 4, of this Sunday edition, a study of which I affirm will prove the statements made by me in regard to the Booth family.

The identification of the tintype picture of St. Helen as that of John Wilkes Booth by Gen. Dana stirred to activity my resting energies and revived my purpose to investigate. I at once began to call for proof of the death of John Wilkes Booth, and began by asking of Dana what evidence they had of the capture and killing of Booth. In reply to this lettter Gen. Dana says, by letter of date December 25, 1897:

"Booth, I personally knew; Herold I did not. After Booth was killed he was brought to the navy yard, and I went on the boat and identified him. But the body was very much thinner and features very much pinched up, as though he had suffered a great deal.

"He was buried near the old jail and a battery of artillery drawn over his grave to obliterate all trace of it."

Thus we have Gen. Dana claiming to identify the body of John Wilkes Booth on the boat in April, 1865, with the reservation that the body was much thinner and features much more pinched up than usual for Booth, and on the 17th day of January, 1898, thirty-three years later, we have Gen. Dana identifying John Wilkes Booth from a tintype picture of St. Helen, claiming to be Booth, taken twelve years after Dana is supposed to have identified the dead body of John Wilkes Booth on the boat. Which identification is CORRECT?

Was it Booth's body on the boat, or was it the living Booth sitting for the picture taken at Glenrose Mills, in Western Texas, twelve years after his

GEN. LEW WALLACE.
One of the Military Court Who Sentenced Mrs. Surratt and
Others to Be Hanged.

EDWIN BOOTH,
At the Age of 31.

dead body is supposed to have lain on the boat at Washington?

This leaves a doubt in the minds of all men who read this state of facts. Under the rule of law in the application of evidence in matters criminal the doubt resolves itself against the truth of the witness and the benefit of the doubt is given to the defendant, Booth. Dana both identifies the supposed body of Booth on the boat and then unquestionably identifies the living Booth from the tintype picture, taken as before stated. This being true, then applying the legal rule as to civil proof, his evidence stands at an equipoise, and under that condition we find in favor of Booth's escape until there is a preponderance of proof to the contrary.

Being advised that Gen. Lew Wallace was the only surviving member of the military court which tried and convicted David E. Herold, Mrs. Surratt and others, by the judgment of which court Herold and Mrs. Surratt were hanged and the others convicted, I wrote under the date of January 25, 1898, calling on Gen. Wallace for the proof which was heard at that court. I also asked for such evidence as was then and now in possession of the government of the United States showing that Booth had been captured and killed.

The General replied as follows:

"Crawfordsville, Ind., Jan. 27, 1898.

"Dear Sir: In reply to yours of the 25th inst., I beg to say that to my certain knowledge John Wilkes Booth was buried under a brick pavement in a room of the old penitentiary prison of Washington City; also that after he had lain buried there for a time, at the request of his friends, his remains were taken up and transferred to Baltimore, where they now lie, under a very handsome marble monument erected to his memory by men of whom I have reason to think as little as I did him. Respectfully yours,

"(Signed.)   LEW WALLACE."

From this man, great in war and greater by far in the literary field of fiction, I expected much valuable proof or suggestions germane to the issue, but the reading of Gen. Wallace's letter can best explain the disappointment it contained in this respect. He speaks positively of his knowledge, without giving the facts on which that knowledge was based—an evasion keen and shrewd, that others might measure the sufficiency of the proofs by his conviction (certain knowledge.) Therefore, in the absence of specific facts, heard by him before a military court, we must rationally conclude that his conviction (certain knowledge) is born of the result of the circum-

174

stantial evidence, the finding of the letters, pictures, etc., belonging to Booth on the supposed body of Booth. A body said to be Booth's was buried, Gen. Wallace says, and subsequently exhumed and transplanted from Washington City at the Old Navy Yard, to the Booth lot in a Baltimore cemetery, and a monument erected to the memory of Booth. These are mere circumstances tending to create the impression that the body so transplanted was that of Booth, but is at best a mere surmise, and in the absence of other and further positive and direct proof does not justify a finding of facts as of certain and personal knowledge.

It will be noticed that Gen. Wallace says that the body of Booth was buried under a "brick pavement in a room of the old penitentiary prison of Washington City," to his "certain knowledge," while Gen. Dana says, and is equally positive of his "certain knowledge," that the "body was buried out in the old Navy Yard, and a battery of artillery run over the grave to obliterate any trace of it." This is a complete contradiction of the statement of Gen. Wallace, based on his "certain knowledge," and this can not be an immaterial mistake merely as to detail between these two gentlemen, because each has stated matters of material physical facts, based on their own knowledge, yet in direct contradiction of each other. Then the question is, Who is right? For if the body was buried as Gen. Wallace says, "under a brick pavement in a room of the old penitentiary prison of Washington City," then it could not have been buried, as Gen. Dana says, "out in the Navy Yard," the grave being obliterated by "running a battery of artillery over it." It was not in the building if it was out in the yard, and not out in the yard if it was in the building. Then, who is RIGHT?

It is a physical impossibility for them both to be correct, but it is possible for them both to be mistaken. And so, in being mistaken, their "certain knowledge" of these facts must fall. To these statements, contradictory as they are, I hold their solemn signed letters, including the statements made, which I thought at the time, and now think, come from among the best sources of information on this subject, yet they are to be further contradicted and worse confounded by the statement of others.

The public press, in referring to the death of the late Wm. P. Wood, of Washington City, said:

"In the passing of the late Wm. P. Wood, in Washington, several weeks ago, there has gone a man whose associations with the central figures in the Lincoln assassination tragedy were of the most intimate character. Col. Wood was of the Secret

Service at the time of the assassination, the thirty-eighth anniversary of which will occur next Tuesday, and was in Cincinnati when President Lincoln was shot. A telegram from Secretary of War Stanton to him requesting him to come to Washington was the first information Col. Wood had that John Wilkes Booth was the assassin of President Lincoln.

"Col. Wood, in speaking of the burial of the body of Booth, said:

" 'The body of Booth was taken off the steamer Ide April 27, 1865, down the Potomac river; from the steamer it was placed on a boat by Capt. Baker and his nephew, a lieutenant in the New York Seventy-first Volnnteers, and carried to an island twenty-seven miles from Washington, and secretly buried there. That story was given out that Booth had been buried under the flagstone in the district jail was only told to keep the public mind at ease and satisfy public curiosity.''

So, while Gen. Wallace and Gen. Dana contradict each other they are both contradicted by Col. Wood, making confusion confounded, while Capt. **E. W.** Hillard, of Metropolis, Illinois, recently published a statement in which he said that he "was one of four privates who carried the remains of Booth from the old Capital Prison in Washington to a gunboat, which carried them about ten miles down the Po-

tomac river, when the body was sunk in the river,"
etc. Therefore, Gen. Dana, Col. Wood and Capt.
Hillard say by their statements that Gen. Wallace is
mistaken. Gen. Wallace, Col. Wood and Capt. Hillard say that Gen. Dana is mistaken, while Col. Wood
and Capt. Hillard say that both Gen. Wallace and
Gen. Dana are mistaken, and Col. Wood and Capt.
Hillard are agreed upon the material points that the
supposed body of John Wilkes Booth was buried in
the Potomac river, differing only in the immaterial
point as to the distance the body was carried down
the river. Therefore, from the weight or preponderance of proof, it appears that the body was buried in the Potomac river. If this was in fact the
body of John Wilkes Booth, why was it secretly and
mysteriously handled around, as shown in these
statements, while the masses of the people of the
United States were clamoring for the avenging of
the death of President Lincoln? What could have
been more satisfactory than for the government to
have made public proffer of the body? This, it
seems, common judgment would have dictated to
the officials then in power. And we believe it
would have been done if in truth and in fact this
body in question had been that of John Wilkes
Booth. And why did not the government in this
instance turn the body over publicly to Booth's

family? This is the custom of the government—State and national—in dealing with their executed dead. This was done in the case of Guitteau, the assassin of President Garfield, and Czolgolsz, the assassin of President McKinley. Why this exception with the body of Booth?

Col. Wood says that the story of the burial of Booth's body at the "Navy Yard was circulated to gratify the people." The people would have been much more gratified at seeing and identifying the body. What mattered it to them where the body of Booth should be buried? They were only anxious to know that Booth was dead. This was the gratification supposed to be desired. The truth is, but one purpose was served, and that the one desired, the concealment of the body claimed to be that of Booth, because it was known that it was not the body of John Wilkes Booth. From the true facts and circumstances as they existed there is neither sense nor reason for any other conclusion.

On the 22d day of January, 1898, I addressed a communication to Mr. H. M. Alsen, editor of Harper's Weekly, giving a full statement of the facts in my possession respecting the escape of Booth, asserting that in my opinion Booth had not in fact been killed, as reported, at the Garrett home in Virginia, in April, 1865, but had made his escape, and I believed Booth then to be alive and at large in the West. Mr. Alsen replied as follows:

"Harper & Brothers—Editorial Rooms,
"Franklin Square, New York,
"January 25, 1898.

"Dear Sir: In reply to your letter of January 22. * * * Of the facts you mention we have not the slightest doubt. The rumor that John Wilkes Booth was still alive frequently reached Edwin Booth, the actor. Yet it was frequently investigated, found false or quietly ignored. Sincerely yours,

"(Signed) H. M. ALSEN, Editor."

And now comes the climax in the shape of a voluntary letter from the United States War Department, as follows:

"War Department,
"Office of the Judge Advocate General,
"Washington, May 13, 1898.

"F. L. Bates, Memphis, Tenn.

"Dear Sir: I am collecting matter for a detailed account of the assassination of President Lincoln by J. Wilkes Booth, and seeing your letter to this department concerning the evidence you therein state you possess, that Booth was not captured and killed by the Federal troops, I have been prompted to write you in my private capacity as a citizen, and not as an employe of the War Department, and inquire if you will kindly give me for publication, if found available, such information on the subject as you may possess.

"While I have not what may be styled direct or positive evidence that the man killed was Booth, I have such circumstantial evidence as would seem to prove the fact beyond doubt. Still, I would be glad to examine any evidence to the contrary.

"Hoping to hear from you soon, I am, very respectfully, your obedient servant,

"(Signed) JOHN P. SIMONTON."

The voluntary statement of Mr. Simonton being true, establishes beyond question the fact that the government has no positive or direct proof of the capture and killing of Booth. Then this explains why the government did not expose the supposed body of Booth. Because they had no conclusive proof of its identity they kept it concealed from the public, for the good effect the deception would have on the public, that they might lull to rest the outraged and restless public sentiment demanding vengeance.

Gen. Wallace refers to the monument to John Wilkes Booth, in Green Mount Cemetery, Baltimore, Maryland, standing in the family lot, the last resting place of the members of the Booth family who have joined the pilgrims in the shadowed valley of the spirit land beyond that river, the boundary line between the dwelling of the living and the home of the dead. It is worthy to mention in this connection that on this monument is chiseled only the name "Booth," and that on the base, the white shaft stands barren of name or epitaph to John Wilkes Booth. Why is this? Does St. Helen's story explain? When the keeper of the Booth lot asked Edwin Booth if the name of John Wilkes Booth, with an epitaph to him, should be placed on the monument, his reply was, "Let it remain blank." By the light of subsequent investigation we understand Edwin Booth's reason for this order. It was in fact not the monument of the dead John Wilkes Booth, as the keeper and the uninformed public believed.

On one occasion a friend asked to speak to Edwin Booth respecting the subject of John Wilkes Booth's crime, when Edwin Booth interrupted him by saying, "Yes, that Washington affair was a horrible crime, but then John Wilkes is my brother." He uttered this with great emotion and ended the subject.

Notice Edwin's unwitting reply, "John Wilkes is my brother," not "John Wilkes was my brother."

To strengthen the theory that Booth had been captured and killed there was a publication in the Baltimore Sun of January 18, 1903, under the head lines:

"WHERE JOHN WILKES BOOTH LIES."

(Published thirty-eight years after the assasination of the President.)

"It is an interesting fact that Edwin Booth never desisted from his potent and quiet endeavor to recover the body of John Wilkes Booth until he delivered it to his mother in Maryland. Of John Wilkes Booth's burial there can be no doubt. John T. Ford, the Baltimore theatrical manager, and Charles B. Bishop, the comedian, both told me that they witnessed for Edwin Booth the exhuming of the body."

(Then we ask where from? Out of the obliterated grave described by Gen. Dana; from under the brick pavement in the room in the old Penitentiary Building described by Wallace, or from the waters of the Potomac river, as described by Col. Wood and Capt. Hillard?) "And that the same was identified and sent to his mother. This should set at rest the rumors that Booth lives."

Of the exhuming of this body and its identification by John T. Ford and Charles B. Bishop, as published by the Baltimore Sun, is incomplete as an historical fact, for the reason that there were others present at the same time with Mr. Ford and Mr. Bishop, who have likewise spoken of the manner of the identification of this body as that of John Wilkes Booth, which was shipped to Baltimore and claimed by some to be the body of John Wilkes Booth. Among the others present was Miss Blanche Chapman, leading lady in the play, "Why Smith Left Home" company, and in referring to the story published in the Baltimore Sun, she says:

"One morning in 1872, just after rehearsal, my godfather, John T. Ford, manager of the theater, came to me and in a strangely serious voice for him to assume when addressing me, said: 'Blanche, keep your eyes and ears open, and your mouth shut, and follow me.' I followed him out through the back of the theater and across the street to Mr. Weaver's undertaking establishment, which was just opposite. He led the way to a sort of private room at the back of the shop, furtherest from the street, and upon entering I saw a number of people seated or standing around a rough, earth-stained box, which contained something that was wrapped in a muddy army blanket. Some of the people present I knew at the time, but there were some I did not know. Of course, I afterward learned their names, and the company was made up as follows: John T. Ford, my godfather and manager of the theater; Charles B. Bishop, the comedian; Mrs. Booth, widow of the elder Booth and mother of Edwin Booth, Junius Brutus Booth, and a still younger brother, whose name I did not know; Mr. Weaver, the undertaker, my little sister and myself.

"It was not long before I began to realize what the solemn little conclave meant. The muddy brown army blanket was partly removed from the object inside of it with a decorous solemnity that I could not misunderstand. Mr. Bishop approached the box, and turning to Junius Brutus Booth, said in a low tone: 'You are sure about that being the only tooth in his head that had been filled?' 'Yes.'

"Mr. Bishop then gently pressed down the lower jaw of the body in the box and with his thumb and forefinger withdrew the tooth indicated. It had been filled with gold, and the peculiar form of the filling was at once recognized by Junius Brutus Booth. Mr. Bishop then carefully drew off one of the long riding boots, which were still on the feet and limbs of the body, which had evidently lain in the earth for years, and as he did so the foot and lower portion of the limb remained in the boot. An examination was then made, and it was plainly seen that the ankle had been fractured. By this time, of course, I realized from what I saw and heard that the remains in the box were those of John Wilkes Booth, returned to the family by the government,"

It will be remembered that President Lincoln was assassinated in the Ford Theater, at Washington, D. C., a place owned by this same John T. Ford, or run by him; that Ford and Bishop were warm personal friends of John Wilkes Booth, and the others were friends of the Booth family, who of all people were anxious that the government officials and the American people at large should believe that John Wilkes Booth, their relative and friend, had been killed. For this belief meant absolute protection for the living John Wilkes Booth at Glenrose Mills, Tex., known as John St. Helen.

Suppose these people had failed to recognize and had announced that the body shown was not that of John Wilkes Booth. The government would have been up in arms, figuratively speaking, and the people of America frenzied with indignation over the deception practiced upon them, would have demanded punishment and justice for the deceivers.

There is no question that there was a body exhumed, or otherwise obtained, at Washington, as stated in the Sun's publication, and as disclosed in the statements of Ford, Bishop and Miss Chapman. But the examination of this body discloses the fact that it was not the body of John Wilkes Booth. The government could not afford to have been caught

red-handed in the act of attempting to palm off a
spurious body on the friends and relatives of John
Wilkes Booth. Therefore the body was kept for
seven years, at the end of which time it was identified by a gold-filled tooth and a limb that came off
in a boot which had been left at the home of Dr.
Mudd seven years before.

It is a physical fact that Dr. Mudd cut one of the
riding boots from the injured limb of Booth on the
morning of April 15, 1865, the limb at that time being so swollen and painful as to render it impossible
for Booth to longer endure the suffering it caused,
and from that time to the date of his supposed capture and burial Booth had on but one riding boot.
And at the time this supposed identification was
being made in Baltimore, as described by Miss Chapman, the very boot said to have been drawn off,
carrying with it the wounded foot and leg, was at
that self-same time in the archives of the government at Washington, where it was placed after being removed from the home of Dr. Mudd. So that
the identification story published in the Baltimore
Sun, the same as described by Blanche Chapman,

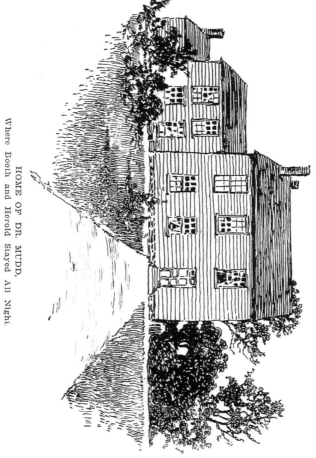

HOME OF DR. MUDD,
Where Booth and Herold Stayed All Night

THE HOME OF DR. MUDD AND THE RIDING BOOT
OF BOOTH.

Which Was Taken Off the Injured Limb of John Wilkes
Booth by Dr. Mudd on the Morning of the 15th of April,
1865, Where It Was Afterward Recovered by the Federal
Troops.

must fall flat, for the reason that the very means of identification accepted as physical facts proving the identity of the exhumed body to be that of John Wilkes Booth, actually prove it to have been the body of some one else who had on two boots.

In this connection I reproduce what Mr. Moxly says in a published interview:

"Mr. Basil Moxly, veteran doorkeeper at John T. Ford's Opera House, after a silence of years, informs the world that the body buried in Green Mount Cemetery, Baltimore, was not that of the assassin, John Wilkes Booth, but that of another man, forwarded to Baltimore by the government at the solicitation of the Booth family and their friends.

"Mr. Moxly is the sole survivor of the men who acted as pall-bearers at what he now terms a 'mock funeral,' and he has deemed the time ripe to tell the facts in this strange disclosure.

" 'I knew Booth well,' said Mr. Moxly, 'and I conversed with him only a short time before the affair in Washington. I am the only one of the pall-bearers left. The man who was brought to Baltimore did not resemble Booth; he had brown hair, while Booth's was jet black; there was also a difference in their general appearance.' "

The statement of Mr. Moxly is positive and conclusive that the body buried at Baltimore was not that of John Wilkes Booth, and the question, "Was John Wilkes Booth killed?" again arises, and we revert back to the evidence held by the government, where we find the circumstance of finding Booth's letters, pictures, check, etc., on the body of the man killed, which John St. Helen, the mysterious cultured gentleman of leisure living at the very edge of civilization, explains were in the possession of the dark-haired, swarthy complexioned man, not quite so tall or large as himself, by the name of Ruddy or Roby, his better recollection being that it was Ruddy or a name sounding the most like the word "Ruddy."

That Ruddy or Roby was the man killed there can no longer be a well-founded doubt, and I leave the submitted facts for reflection while taking up the most interesting part of Booth's life in the West, the home of the Indian, the Mexican and the cowboy.

CHAPTER XIII.

A BALTIMOREAN STILL.

Baltimore has the distinction of being the chief stage upon which Booth played his romantic part as an actor, where the footlights separated him from the people, and from that city of beautiful and cultured women and honorable and intellectual men John Wilkes Booth drank the inspiration that made him famous as an actor, and that made him ever the courteous and cultured gentleman during his wandering life on the Western plains. For Baltimore and her people he carried and cherished in his memory, love and gratitude and honor to the hour he commanded his heart "Be still."

He had often said to me: "In the morning of my life the star of my fate rose from without the firmament of Baltimore's elite, and I love and honor her."

How vividly do I recall his proud and haughty, yea, his beautiful and defiant face, when he spoke of Baltimore, the home of his youth and early manhood, and the Baltimorean as his friend. And you of Baltimore who remember him in his strength and honor, this greeting I send as a message from him, from his home nearer the gateway of the Day, where twillight greets the evening star, where darkness makes of ours a dreamland and of the Orient a land of day: "John Wilkes Booth's fondest memories are of thee and of his friends in Baltimore."

The life of John Wilkes Booth is, however, certainly no less, and perhaps far more interesting, in the part he played on the Western plains, on the stage by Nature set, in which he had before him the wild man and the semi-civilized people of this wild section as an appreciative audience. And while there are doubtless many residents of the Monumental City who treasure up reminiscences of Booth's bright youth and splendid, misguided genius, there live today thousands of people on the plains who cherish his memory and love his personality without a knowledge of his true name, his crime or his wasted genius, and would, like the cowboy, build a monument to his memory.

Of John Wilkes Booth his brother, Edwin, himself a genius and a judge, said: "He has the genius of my father, and is more gifted than I," while Joe Jefferson, the "Rip Van Winkle" of all ages, with whom the world laughed or wept at his will, saw John Wilkes Booth in the last years before his insane deed at Washington and told me that he never saw so great a performance as his impersonation of "Richard III." In "Richard III." he played under the name of John Wilkes, and never used his surname until he played Horatio to Edwin Booth's Hamlet. When for the first time his name was given on the bills as John Wilkes Booth, at the close of the play, as usual, the call came for Edwin Booth, and as the curtain went up Edwin Booth came down the stage leading his brother, John Wilkes Booth, by the arm and, pointing to him, said:

"I think he has done well, don't you?"

Then came from the audience cries of "Yes!" "Yes!" and tumultuous applause.

Mr. Jefferson said: "John Wilkes Booth was a little taller than his brother Edwin, possessed his intellectual and beautiful eyes, with great symmetry of features, and an especially fine forehead and curly, black hair.''

''He was as handsome as a Greek god,'' says Mr. Edwin M. Delfind. Continuing further, he said: ''It is saying a good deal, but he was a much handsomer man than his brother Edwin. He possessed a voice much like his brother's—melodious, sweet, full and strong, and was a consummate elocutionist. He was a great admirer of those Greek and Roman characters that are deemed exponents of popular liberty and heroic patriotism. In these he went almost to radicalism. Of the Brutuses he was an especial devotee, and I shall never forget his recitation of Brutus' speech in ''Julius Caesar,'' of his defiance in his share of the asssassination, and with what force he rolled out those lines:

'' 'My ancestors did from the streets of Rome the tarquin drive.'

''He said that of all Shakespeare's characters, 'I like Brutus the best, excepting only Lear.' There is no doubt but that the study of these characters and meditation upon their deeds had much to do with shaping that mental condition which led to the murder of President Lincoln.

"I was talking with Edwin Booth at the Players one day and remarked to him: 'Mr. Booth, there is an incident in the nation's history to which I would like to allude.' He promptly comprehended, and replied with flashing eyes and compressed lips, 'You mean that affair at Washington. I could not approve of what John Wilkes did, and would rather not discuss it. He is my brother.'

"As to the dramatic genius of John Wilkes Booth, I can speak with professional authority. It was of the highest order, and had he continued on the stage his fame and success would have equaled that of his father. The father I never saw, but nearly every great actor from Edwin Forrest down to the present day I have seen and heard, and with the exception of Forrest and that brilliant, erratic genius, Edwin Adams, John Wilkes Booth's genius excelled them all.

"As I have said, he was a great admirer of Lear. I don't think his genius would ever have made his rendering of the part equal to Forrest. Lear and Booth genius were not quite in harmony. He did not have the large physical proportions essential to

the performance of Shakespeare's sublimest charac-
ters. Edwin Forrest did, and was the only Lear the
stage has ever seen. But Booth was unequalled as
Richard III., and would have made the greatest
Hamlet, Cassius, Othello, Macbeth, Cornelius and
Charles Moore, as well as other similar parts.

"In plays like 'The Taming of the Shrew' he had
achieved distinction. He acted in such parts with
a brilliant dash and sweep that were irresistible to
women. He was an imperious fascinator and
women idolized him.

"Once in Philadelphia, when going over with Mr.
Forrest his 1623d edition of Shakespeare, I expressed
to him my admiration of his Lear. Forrest flushed
and said: 'Sir, I act Hamlet, but I am Lear.' It is
lamentable that through the insanity which led to
the dark deed in Washington the genius of John
Wilkes Booth was lost to the American stage. His
star went out in the darkest night through a deed
that cost the South its best friend, Abraham Lincoln.''

Clara Morris, the emotional actress, now nearing
the last scenes in the playhouse of Time, says of

CLARA MORRIS.
As Sister Genevieve in "The Two Orphans."

JOSEPH JEFFERSON.
As He Appeared at the Interview With Mr. Bates at the
Gayoso Hotel, Memphis, Tennessee.

John Wilkes Booth: "In glancing back over two crowded and busy seasons one figure stands out with clearness and beauty. In this case, so far as my personal knowledge goes, there is nothing derogatory to dignity or manhood in being called 'beautiful,' for he was that bud of splendid promise blasted to the core before its full triumphant blooming, known to the world as a madman and an assassin, but to the profession as 'that unhappy boy, John Wilkes Booth.' He was so young, so bright, so kind.

"I could not have known him well? Of course, too, there are two or three different people in every man's skin. Yet, when we remember that stars are not generally in the habit of showing their brightest, their best side, to the company at rehearsals, we can not help feeling both respect and liking for the one who does.

"There are not many men who can receive a gash over the eye in the scene at night without at least a momentary outburst of temper, but when the combat between Richard and Richmond was being rehearsed, John Wilkes Booth had again and again urged McCullom—that six-foot tall and handsome

man, who entrusted me with the care of his watch
during such encounters, 'To come on hard, come on
hot, old fellow! Harder, faster!' that he would take
the chances of a blow if only they could make a hot
fight of it. Mr. McCullom, who was a cold man at
night, became nervous in his efforts to act like a
fiery one. He forgot that he had struck the full
number of hard blows, and when Booth was expecting a thrust, McCullom, wielding his sword with both
hands, brought it down with awful force fair across
Booth's-forehead. A cry of horror rose, for in one
moment his face was marked in blood, one eyebrow
was clearly cut through. Then came simultaneously
one deep groan from Richard (Booth) and an
exclamation of 'Oh! Good God! Good God!' from
Richmond (McCullom), who stood trembling like a
leaf and staring at his work. Booth, flinging the
blood from his eyes with his left hand, said as gently
as a man could speak: 'That is all right. That is
all right, old man. Never mind me. Only come on
hard, for God's sake, and save the fight!' which he
resumed at once. And though he was perceptibly
weakened it required the sharp order of Mr. Ellsler

to ring the first curtain bell to force him to bring the fight to a close, a single blow shorter than usual. And there was a running to and fro with ice and vinegar, and raw steak, and raw oysters, and when the doctor had placed a few stitches where they were most required Booth laughingly declared that there was provisions enough in the room to start a restaurant.

"McCullom came to try to apologize, to explain, but Booth would have none of it. He held out his hand, saying, 'Why, old fellow, you look as if you had lost the blood—don't worry—now, if my eye had gone, that would have been bad.' And so, with light words he turned to set the unfortunate man at ease, and though he must have suffered much mortification as well as pain from the eye, he never made a sign showing it.

"John Wilkes Booth, like his next elder brother, was rather lacking in height, but his head and throat and the manner of their rising from his shoulders were truly beautiful. His coloring was unusual, the ivory pallor of his skin, the inky blackness of his dusky, thick, curly hair, the heavy lids of his glow-ing eyes, were all Oriental, and they gave a touch of mystery to his face when it fell into gravity, but there was generally a flash of white teeth behind his black, silky mustache.

"Now, it is scarcely exaggerating to say that the fair sex were in love with John Wilkes Booth, or John Booth, as he was called, the name Wilkes being apparently unknown to his family and close friends. I played with John Wilkes, to my great joy, playing 'Player Queen,' and in 'The Marble Heart,' I was one of the group of three statues in the first act, then a girl in my teens.

"With all my admiration for the person and the genius of John Wilkes Booth, his crime I can not condone. The killing of that homely, tender-hearted father, Abraham Lincoln, a rare combination of courage, justice and humanity, whose death at the hands of an actor will be a grief of horror and shame to the profession forever. And yet I cannot believe that John Wilkes Booth was the leader of a band of bloody conspirators.

"Who shall draw the line and say, 'Here genius ends and madness begins?' There was that touch of strangeness, in Edwin it was a profound melancholy; in John it was an exaggeration of spirit, almost a madness. There was the natural vanity of the actor, too, who craves a dramatic selection in real life. There was also his passionate love and sympathy for the South, which was easier to be played on than a pipe.

"Undoubtedly he conspired to kidnap the President; that would appeal to him. But after that I truly believe he was a tool; certainly he was no leader. Those who led him knew his courage, his belief in fate, his loyalty to his friends, and because they knew these things he drew the lot, as it was meant he should from the first. Then, half mad, he accepted the part fate cast him for and committed the murderous crime.

> 'God moves in a mysterious way
> His wonders to perform.'

" 'And God shutteth not up His mercies forever in displeasure.' We can only shiver and turn our thoughts away from the bright light that went out in such utter darkness. Poor, guilty, unhappy John Wilkes Booth!''

A BALTIMOREAN STILL.

These extensive quotations are made from the two veterans of the stage, Clara Morris and Edwin M. Delfind, the personal friends of John Wilkes Booth, whose long acquaintance and association with him enabled them to write these articles, showing the characteristics, personal appearance and ability of John Wilkes Booth, whom they so perfectly describe. And yet these descriptions, so true in detail, so perfectly describe John St. Helen, the mysterious gentleman of the plains, who so persistently maintained to me that he was John Wilkes Booth, of whom they had never heard, and that too, thirty-eight years after they are presumed to know that John Wilkes Booth is dead. This is wonderful and unanswerable proof that the John St. Helen whom I knew was actually the John Wilkes Booth whom they knew and describe, as he claimed to be.

In this connection it is of interest to know something more of John Wilkes Booth's father, the famous actor, Junius Brutus Booth, Sr., who came to the United States from England, and followed the profession in this country with such success that for all time links the name of Booth with the American stage.

JOHN WILKES BOOTH, AGED 38.
The Picture Taken at Glenrose Mills, Texas, on the Bosque
River. (A reproduction from the tin-type.)

JUNIUS BRUTUS BOOTH, THE FIRST.
Father of John Wilkes Booth, as Sir Giles Overreach, Showing the Famous Actor in One of His Favorite Characters.

Booth, the elder, acted because he loved to act, and was farmer because he loved to farm; which of the two he liked best seemed always a matter of doubt to himself and naturally became so with others. He was eminently successful in both farming and acting, his great reputation as an actor being made after he came to America, where he stood pre-eminently at the head of his profession. He was a well-read man, with a remarkable talent for showing it. Personally he was dark, had strong eyes, a fine mouth and a positive manner. He was a kindly man and lived up to the customs of his time and profession, maintaining all conventional distinctions. Mr. Booth's Baltimore residence was in Exeter street, and his farm was in Belair, about fourteen miles from Baltimore. His professional habits were not unlike those of the late Joseph Jefferson; he played when he felt like it, and when he was not acting he was farming, while he farmed throughout all his engagements in the city of Baltimore.

Be it said to the lasting credit of Mr. Booth that his opinion of himself was much inferior to that entertained of him by others, who thought him pre-eminently the greatest actor of his time, and he has not been equalled by any one since his day.

The likeness of John Wilkes Booth to his father is striking at the age of twenty-seven. But note the more striking resemblance of John Wilkes Booth to his father where he reaches the age of thirty-eight years. This picture is a reproduction of the little tintype picture taken of John St. Helen (John Wilkes Booth) twelve years after the assassination of President Lincoln and Booth's reported capture and death.

CHAPTER XIV.

INFORMING THE WAR DEPARTMENT THAT BOOTH LIVES.

Being convinced that John St. Helen was actually John Wilkes Booth, I determined to locate him, and with this purpose in view I addressed a letter to a personal friend, a lawyer, at Grandberry, Texas, receiving this reply:

"Grandberry, Texas, September 21st, 1898.
"N. L. Cooper & Sons, Attorneys at Law.
F. L. Bates:—

"Dear Sir and Friend—I have made many inquiries about the latter end of St. Helen, if he should have crossed the Jordan, but can make but little discovery. L. B. McClannahan, who was in partnership with A. P. Gordon, in the whiskey business, on the south side of the square, now lives at Bluffdale, eighteen miles southwest from here, on the railroad in Erath county, may know something of St. Helen; also William Farmwalt, whose address is Maryfa, Presideo county, Texas, and G. W. Calvin, Kerrville, Texas.

"It might be that John H. Traylor, formerly of this place, whom you knew, and now mayor of Dallas, Texas, might known something of his whereabouts. I will continue to inquire of any one whom I shall meet that might know of him. Capt. J. J. Farr, whom you remember, now lives at Glenrose Mills, Texas, twenty miles south of this place, and may know something of him. I will see him soon and will then make inquiry.

"Many thanks for your appreciation of myself and family. With high regards for you and yours, I am ever your friend,

(Signed)   "N. L. COOPER."

The result of this investigation located St. Helen at Leadville, Colorado, in October, 1879. From Leadville I traced him to Fresno, California, where he seems merely to have passed through the town.

In the meantime I also sought to investigate the men who had aided Booth to escape and to locate, as far as possible, their identity. With this end in view I addressed a letter to a law firm in Fredericksburg, Virginia, which elicited the following reply:

"Law Office of

"John L. Marye and St. George R. Fitzhugh.

"Fredericksburg, Virginia, October 5th, 1898.

"F. L. Bates, Memphis, Tenn.

"Dear Sir—Your favor received. Major or Lieutenant M. B. Ruggles is with Arnold, Caeslable & Co., New York City. Major Edward S. Ruggles, the brother of M. B. Ruggles, is a farmer in King George county, Virginia. Gen. Daniel Ruggles, the father of the three gentlemen, died here about a year ago, and his widow is living here now. Very truly yours, etc.,

    (Signed)   "ST. GEORGE R. FITZHUGH."

"Alexandria, Virginia, ————, 1898.

"Capt. Jett was well known and acquainted in Carlin county, Virginia. He was a near relative of mine, with whom I was on the most intimate terms. He went to Baltimore a year after the assassination of President Lincoln, engaged in the business of traveling constantly in Virginia, and married the daughter of a prominent physician of Baltimore. No one blamed him for piloting the Federal Cavalry to where he had left Booth, or criticised him for his efforts to assist Booth in his escape. Sixteen years after he settled in Baltimore he was attacked with paresis, and died at the hospital of Williamsburg, Virginia, repsected by all who knew him.

(Signed.) "JOHN L. MARYE."

Lieut. A. R. Bainbridge, after the close of the war, went to New York City and entered business. Jett, Bainbridge and Ruggles were the members of Mosby's Confederate command who met Booth and Harold at the Rappahannock ferry, and described Booth as wearing at this time a black slouch hat, well pulled down on his forehead, the lame foot was entirely free from covering except a black sock. The crutch or stick which he carried was rough and ungainly. They further say, speaking of the following afternooon: "After we had crossed Booth to the Garrett farm we saw the Federal troops across the Rappahannock river, and we (Ruggles and Bainbridge) were pursued by them, when we fled straight to the Garrett farm and notified Booth to leave, directing him to go into the wooded ravine, which we pointed out to him, over and beyond the Garrett farm, for which place he left at once, carrying a heavy stick in his hand to support his lame leg.''

Through inquiry of a person now in Washington City, whose name it would be an abuse of confidence to disclose, I learned that there was a large family of people by the name of Ruddy living within the immediate neighborhood of Samuel Cox, on the Potomac river, where Booth was secreted, so that I take it the man killed at the Garrett farm was ''Ruddy'' and not ''Roby,'' as several of the men of the Ruddy family answer the description Booth gave of the man who got his letters, pictures, check, etc.

The statements of these gentlemen, Jett, Ruggles and Bainbridge, corroborate St. Helen's story that he (Booth) was met by these gentlemen, Confederate soldiers, at the Rappahannock ferry. Could this have been an incident? Surely it was prearranged. These gentlemen say: ''We met Booth at the ferry,'' but do not say by accident, a mere casualty and seemingly it was by appointment, at a stated time; they had arrived at the ferry in advance of Booth, as if to receive and protect him on his arrival.

Neither Booth nor Herold could have gone to arrange this appointment. Booth was lame and Herold did not know the country in that direction, so remained with Booth, who was suffering a great deal. There can be no well founded doubt but that Ruddy went in advance and made this appointment as detailed to me by St. Helen (Booth).

After successfully locating St. Helen (Booth) at Leadville and later at Fresno, California, I was reasonably sure he still lived and could be located, and supposing it to be a matter of interest to the United States government, I addressed the following letter to the War Department:

"Law Office of F. L. BATES,

"297 Second Street,

"Memphis, Tenn., January 17th, 1898.
"Secretary of War, Washington, D. C.

"Dear Sir—Would it be a matter of any importance to develop the fact to the War Department of the United States that John Wilkes Booth, the assassin of President Lincoln, was not captured and killed by the Federal troops, as is supposed?

"By accident I have been placed in possession of such facts as are conclusive that John Wilkes Booth now lives, and have kept the matter from publication until I have communicated with the War Department of this government. Very truly yours,
"F. L. BATES."

In reply the following endorsements were made on this letter and returned to me, viz.:

First endorsement:

"Office of the Secretary of War Department.
"January 19th, 1898.

(294)   "Memphis, Tenn., Jan. 17th, 1898.

"F. L. Bates says that he is in possession of such facts as are conuclusive that John Wilkes Booth was not captured and killed by the Federal troops, and asks if War Department would consider the matter of enough importance to develop that fact.

"JUDGE ADVOCATE GENERAL."

Second endorsement:

(3808)   "War Department,
"Judge Advocate General's Office,
"Washington, D. C.
January 21st, 1898.

"Respectfully returned to the Secretary of War.

"This is a request by F. L. Bates, of Memphis, Tenn., for information as to whether it would be a matter of importance to develop the fact to the War Department that John Wilkes Booth was not captured and killed by the Federal troops.

"He says that by accident he has recently been placed in possession of such facts as are conclusive.

"It is recommended that he be informed that the matter is of no importance to the War Department.

(Signed)   G. NORMAN LIEBER,

"Judge Advocate General."

"Received back War Department January 22d, 1898.

(294)   "Assistant Secretary."

(L. S. S.)

Third endorsemen

"War Department.

"January 25th, 1898.

"Respectfully returned to Mr. F. L. Bates, No. 272 Second street, Memphis, Tenn., inviting attention to the foregoing report of the Judge Advocate General of the Army.

(Signed) "G. D. MICKLEJOHN,
"Acting Secretary of War."

In view of the fact that the War Department would take no action upon the information furnished of the then living Booth, on January 19th, January 21st and January 25th, 1898, notwithstanding that the officials of the War Department were fully advised that there was no positive or direct proof on file with the government as to the. death of John Wilkes Booth, as is fully shown by the letter of John P. Simonton, of the War Department, of date May 11th, 1898, almost five months later, I ask then why should these officials refuse to investigate the proof of these facts when offered? It must, therefore, follow that the officials, having only circumstantial proof of the death of Booth, did not want and refused to consider proof of the fact that Booth still lived, and went so far as to say that it was a matter of no importance to the War Department to establish the truth that Booth was not killed, as supposed, or that he was still alive.

Does such a declaration, coming as an official finding of the War Department, assist in and perpetuate the escape of Booth, the assassin of President Lincoln? For to officially find that it was a matter of no importance to ascertain whether Booth still lived and was at large when proof was offered to this end was to officially find that John Wilkes Booth should go at large so far as these officials were concerned, notwithstanding the great crime that Booth had committed and its national significance, demanding national reparation.

These officers will not be heard to explain by saying that they did not regard the tender of proof of sufficient importance to justify an investigation. For if it did not justify an official investigation to learn the truth of the statement made it did not justify a finding that it was a matter of no importance to the government whether Booth in fact lived or was dead, which is the logical and unmistakable finding of the War Department, and this finding by these officials in view of the following order, which is yet valid and subsisting, is remarkable to a degree unexplainable:

"War Department,
"Washington, D. C.
April 20th, 1865.

"ONE HUNDRED THOUSAND DOLLARS REWARD.

"The murderer of our late beloved President, Abraham Lincoln, is still at large. Fifty thousand dollars' reward will be paid by this department for his apprehension. In addition to reward offered by municipal authorities or State executives, liberal rewards will be paid for any information that shall conduce to the arrest of either Booth or his accomplices.

"All persons harboring or secreting the said persons, or either of them, or aiding or assisting their concealment or escape, will be treated as accomplices in the murder of the President, and shall be held to trial before a military commission and the punishment of death.

"Let the stain of innocent blood be removed from the land by the arrest and punishment of the murderers. All good citizens are exhorted to aid public justice on this account; every man should consider his own conscience charged with this solemn duty, and rest neither night nor day until it is accomplished.

(Signed)   "EDWIN M. STANTON,
"Secretary of War."

The above order constituted then and constitutes now the national law of the United States respecting the subject of which it treats, and is today and at all times prior to the present day, since its promulgation in 1865, a part of the records of the War Department, the mandates and knowledge of which is chargeable to the officials of the War Department.

G. Norman Lieber, Judge Advocate General of the Army, and Acting Secretary of War Micklejohn, are chargeable with notice and held responsible for its execution; and if, in view of this knowledge, the finding of Micklejohn, Secretary of War, on the 25th day of January, 1898, rescinds the order of Secretary Stanton of April 20th, 1865, it sets free, so far as the War Department could, the assassin of President Lincoln

It stands as a matter of history that at about the hour of four o'clock in the afternoon of April 14th, 1865, General C. C. Augur ordered the guards called in from the protection of the life of President Lincoln, then known to be threatened and in imminent danger, as stated by General Dana, and that at ten minutes past ten o'clock that same evening the President was assassinated, and at thirty minutes past ten, twenty minutes later, the Federal guards, still on duty, opened the gates for Booth, the assassin, to pass out over the East Potomac bridge. So that within six hours after the order of Gen. Augur the President had been shot and the criminal had escaped through the Federal lines, his escape having been made possible by the order of Gen. Augur, whether designedly or not the result was the same, and on the 25th day of January, 1898, thirty-three years later, the officials of the War Department find that proof of the fact that John Wilkes Booth lived and was still at large was of no importance to their department, nor to the Department of Justice of the United States—otherwise proper reference would have been made, and the Department of Justice officially notified instead of finding against an investigation of the facts submitted.

Does this finding against an investigation of the facts offered, proof of the truth that Booth was not captured and killed—make void the order of Secretary Stanton on April 20th, 1865? If not, then is the Acting Secretary of War, as well as the Judge Advocate General, under the provisions of this order, guilty of assisting, by concealment, the escape of John Wilkes Booth.

But, if the finding of January 25th, 1898, of the War Department is a revocation of the order of the War Department of April 20th, 1865, do such acts of these officials make them accessories after the fact, as at common law?

These charges, though grave, are justified by the solemn records which I hold as physical evidence of the charges made, and I appeal to the American people for a verdict on the issues thus joined as an expiation for the murder of Abraham Lincoln, *whose death is yet unavenged!*

Not being satified with the disposition of this matter by the War Department, I turned to the State Department, addressing a latter to Secretary John Hay, stating in substance the facts which I had submitted to the War Department, and received the following letter in reply:

"Department of State,
"Washington, D. C.

April 27th, 1900.

"F. L. Bates.

"Dear Sir—The Secretary of State requests me to acknowledge receipt of your favor of the 24th of April and to thank you for it. Very respectfully,

(Signed) "E. J. BABCOCK,

"Private Secretary."

This closed my efforts at presenting the matter of Booth's discovery to the government of the United States. And at last of what interest was the matter to Secretary of State John Hay, the pride of the American people—the world's greatest diplomat?

In this connection, however, it will be of interest to note what Secretary Hay, in January, 1890, had to say relative to John Wilkes Booth and his escape:

"Booth was a young man of twenty-six, strikingly handsome, with a pale olive face, dark eyes, and that ease and grace of manner which came to him by right from his theatrical ancestry. (How strikingly like St. Helen.) Booth in his flight gained the Navy Yard bridge (East Potomac bridge) in a few minutes, and was allowed to pass the guards, and shortly afterward Herold came on the bridge and was allowed to pass; a moment later the owner of the horse which Herold rode came up in pursuit of his animal, and he, the only honest man of the three, was turned back by the guards.

"If Booth had been in health there is no reason why he should not have remained at large a long while. He might even have made his escape to some foreign country, though sooner or later a crime so prodigious will generally find its perpetrator out. But it is easy to hide among sympathizing people; many a Union soldier escaping from prison has walked hundreds of miles through the enemy's country, relying implicitly upon the friendship of the negroes. Booth, from the time he crossed the Navy

Yard (East Potomac) bridge, received the assistance of a large number of men. With such devoted assistance Booth might have wandered a long way, but there was no final escape save suicide for an assassin.''

These comments on the possibilities of Booth's escape by one of the wise, if not in fact the wisest, diplomats known to the civilized world, challenges attention; in fact, was prophetic and (as subsequent events disclosed), is paralleled only by the prophets of old.

Hay says, ''from the nature of things Booth could have escaped, * * * but there was no final escape save suicide for the assassin.'' Who will deny the correctness of his prophecy, since Booth did escape, remained in hiding thirty-eight years and did suicide? It was this power of foreseeing the possibility of coming events that made Secretary Hay **the** greatest of diplomats.

CHAPTER XV.

GEN. ALBERT PIKE IDENTIFIES BOOTH.

While trying to trace Booth after he left Fresno, California, I read a story from Col. Edward Levan, of Monterey, Mexico. He says that a man whom he believed to be Booth roomed with him during the winter of 1868, in Lexington, Kentucky. The two became quite friendly, and Col. Levan openly declared to the man, who was going by the name of J. J. Marr, that he believed him to be John Wilkes Booth. Mr. Marr did not deny the allegation, but shortly thereafter left Lexington, where he was "playing the character of a lawyer."

Col. Levan says that he afterward learned that Mr. Marr had settled at Village Mills, Texas, and from there went to Glenrose Mills, Texas, at which place I first met John St. Helen, and where he declared himself to be John Wilkes Booth.

Col. M. W. Connolly, a distinguished newspaper man, at present and for many years past connected

GEN. ALBERT PIKE.

The Veteran Mason, Statesman, Lawyer and Poet, as He
Appeared at the Time of His Recognition of John Wilkes
Booth at Fort Worth, Texas, in 1885.

Booth (as D. E. George) Playing the Role of a House Painter,
and the Only Painting Job He Ever Did.

with the leading papers as editor-in-chief, a gentleman of the highest type, a brilliant writer and a man
of honor and integrity, says:

"I am strongly inclined to believe that David E.
George, who died at Enid, Oklahoma Territory, was
John Wilkes Booth, the man who killed Lincoln.

"In 1883, while in the little town of Village Mills,
Texas, I met George, although I never knew his
name, and cannot say whether he went under that
name or not. He impressed me. I had seen Edwin
Booth once in Galveston, and had some knowledge
of the appearance of the Booth family. Later I went
to Fort Worth as editor of the Gazette, under the
late Walter Malone. I had forgotten all about my
casual acquaintance of Village Mills.

"One night I was in the Pickwick Hotel barroom
talking to Gen. Albert Pike, who had come down
from Washington on legal business. I had called on
him to inquire about a claim against the government
in which he was interested—the claim of the heirs
of my wife's grandfather, Major Michie, of La-
Grange, Tennessee, whose cotton and cotton gins
were burned by the Federal troops when Grant was

at LaGrange. Capt. Day, of Day & Maas, proprietors, was behind the bar. It was in 1884 or 1885, and we were unconventional then.

"Tom Powell, mayor of Fort Worth, joined us, and Temple Houston, youngest son of the ex-Governor of Tennessee, the man who whipped Santa Anna at San Jacinto, and the first president of the Texas republic (Gen Sam Houston), was there. I was about to leave, was waiting for a pause in order to excuse myself; Gen. Pike was explaining how he had been credited with the authorship of 'The Old Canoe,' which he said was written by some woman; just then my Village Mills friend came in accompanied by some one, I think Long Scurlock, who used to edit the Chronicle at Cleburne, Texas. Capt. Day turned to make a change. I was watching Gen. Pike closely (trying to get away), when suddenly he threw up his hands, his face white as his hair and beard, and exclaimed:

" 'My God! John Wilkes Booth!' He was much excited, trembled like an aspen, and at my suggestion went to his room. He seemed weakened by the shock, the occasion of which I could not realize at the moment. I saw him climb the stairs to his room and turned to look for my Village Mills acquaintance, but could not find him.

"While talking to Temple Houston the next morning I pointed out my Village Mills friend when I was called to Gen. Pike, who was standing on the opposite side of the street, and Temple Houston promised me that he would look the man up and get a story. I have heard that the alleged Booth, the man whom I had met, moved to the Territory later, but I took no newspaper interest in the matter.

"I never saw J. Wilkes Booth, but I have seen his pictures, and while I am in no way certain, I am strongly of the belief that the man who died at Enid was John Wilkes Booth. I am quite sure that the venerable author of 'Every Year' believed it was the infatuated actor, and I am sure that he was amazed to find that his bewailment, 'There are fewer to regret us,' did not include the man who took a leading part in our great national tragedy."

It is of interest in this connection to state that Fort Worth, Texas, is only about forty-fives miles to the northeast of Grandberry, Texas, my old home and St. Helen's. It was from this place, in 1878, that he drifted to Leadville, Colorado, and from thence to Fresno, California, and was next seen—in 1884 or 1885—at Fort Worth, Texas, near his old home, by Gen. Albert Pike, in company with M. W. Connolly, and by Gen. Pike recognized as John Wilkes Booth.

The man supposed to be Booth was seen by others before he settled at Glenrose Mills, for Dr. H. W. Gay says:

"I knew John Wilkes Booth in 1857, and while I was at Fort Donaldson, a prisoner of war, the news was flashed over the world that President Lincoln had been slain by John Wilkes Booth. I was horrified to think of such a thing, for Booth, though a boy when I knew him, in appearance was the most accomplished gentleman with whom I had ever come in contact. All who knew him well were captivated by him. He was the most hospitable, genial fellow to be met, and when drinking or much in company, he was always quoting Shakespeare, or some other poet. How many times have I seen him strike a tragic attitude and exclaim:

" 'The aspiring youth who fires the Ephesians dome
Outlives in fame the pious fools who reared it.'

"I read of his capture and death and never
doubted it until the year 1869. I was then living in
what is now Tate county, Mississippi. One evening
about dusk a man came to my house claiming that
he was one of the Ku-Klux Clan run out of Arkansas
by Clayton's militia (the Clayton referred to being
Powell Clayton, until recently Ambassador to Mexico).

"I soon recognized this man as an erratic fellow.
During his stay at my house he told me that John
Wilkes Booth was not killed, but made his escape
and spent a short while in Mexico with Maximillan's
army, but got into trouble, and his life was saved
by reason of the fact that he was a Catholic. The
man also stated that during Booth's short stay in
Mexico he had lived in disguise as an itinerant Catholic priest. He also told me the story of how Booth
had escaped after the assassination was done, and it
corresponded exactly with Mr. Bates' story as told
by John St. Helen, even to the crossing of the Mississippi river at Catfish Point and going thence up

the Arkansas river to Indian Territory. And that Booth afterward met Junius Brutus Booth and his mother in San Francisco.''

This meeting was possibly arranged while John Wilkes Booth was in the Indian Territory, and may explain in some measure his employment to drive a team from Nebraska City, Nebraska, to Salt Lake, Utah, for Mr. L. Treadkel, in 1866 or 1867, and his unceremonious desertion of duty before reaching Salt Lake City.

So we have Booth, or St. Helen, meeting his oldest brother, Junius Brutus Booth, at San Francisco in 1866 or 1867. Again we locate him in Lexington, Kentucky, in company with Col. Levan, in 1868 or 1869, and seen by Dr. Gay in Tate county, Mississippi, in 1869. In 1872 I met and knew him intimately at Glenrose Mills, Texas. In 1883 Mr. Connolly saw him at Village Mills, Texas, and again in 1884 or 1885 at Fort Worth, Texas, where he was recognized by Gen. Albert Pike.

At Fort Worth we lost sight of Booth for a number of years, but it seems from the best obtainable information that he drifted into the vicinity of Guthrie, Oklahoma Territory, but was located at Hennessy, Oklahoma Territory, in the year 1896, playing the role of a gentleman of leisure, under the name of George D. Ryan, where he remained until some time in the year 1899, when he located at El Reno, Oklahoma Territory, sixty-five miles south of Hennessy, stopping at the Anstein hotel, where he was domiciled in 1898 when I took up the matter with the government authorities at Washington.

On moving to El Reno, in 1899, Booth made deposits of money, opening an account with the State bank of that place, under the name of David E. George. Assuming the character of a journeyman house painter he took a contract and painted a small cottage for Mr. Anstien, the proprietor of the Anstein hotel, and advertised himself as David E. George, house painter, in the Daily Democrat, a newspaper published at El Reno, but took no jobs of painting after that first one for Mr. Anstien, and did no other work in this nor any other business at El Reno.

At the El Reno State bank, where Booth made his deposits as David E. George, the tintype picture of

St. Helen (Booth), taken twelve years after the assassination of President Lincoln, was at once identified by the officials of the bank as being a true likeness of the man David E. George, who made the deposits at their bank and with whom they were personally acquainted. At the request of Mr. Bellamy, one of the bank officials, I went with him to another bank, the name of which I do not now remember, and was introduced to the president of this bank, whose name I believe was Dr. Davis, who at once identified the tintype picture of St. Helen as a true and correct likeness of David E. George.

After remaining at the Anstien Hotel for quite a long while David E. George (Booth) bought a cottage at El Reno, paying thirty-five hundred dollars for it, where he installed a family by the name of Simmons, who were to board him for the rent of the place. He told the Anstiens that he was tired of hotel life and requested them to look for a wife for him, saying in a joking way that he would pay handsomely for one well suiting his fancy, who would be willing to take charge of his cottage home.

Mrs. Simmons also took to board with her the Methodist minister and his wife, the Rev. and Mrs. Harper. Mr. Harper is a man of means and follows the ministry as a matter of choice and not as a means of livelihood, and his wife is a lady of great refinement and culture, occupying in church and social circles a high position. Being thrown much together in the ordinary course of everyday life at the cottage Mrs. Harper as well as the members of the Simmons family grew to be on intimate terms with George (Booth), who fell ill with his chronic asthmatic affliction, from which he suffered a great deal, and was removed from his cottage home to the Kerfoot Hotel. Mrs. Harper, Mrs. Simmons and other kind-hearted ladies of the city visited George (Booth), who by right of birth and breeding moved in the social circle to which he was born, regardless of his advertisement in the Democrat as a house painter, performing for him such ministries as were necessary.

Mrs. Harper makes the following statement:

"Mr. George (Booth) had been a resident of the Territory for several years. He had always been well supplied with money, the origin or source of which no one knew, for from some mysterious source he received a regular remittance. He was a familiar figure in Guthrie, El Reno and Enid. My acquaintance with Mr. George led me to believe him to be a very different person from what he represented himself to be as David E. George, the painter. He was eccentric, and though he claimed to be a painter of houses, yet he did no work. He was possessed of the highest degree of intelligence, had always the bearing of a gentleman of cultivation and refinement, and in conversation was fluent and captivating, while he discussed subjects of the greatest moment with learning, familiarity and ease. There were very few people with whom he cared to associate. Generally he was gloomy, though at times he would brighten up, sing snatches of stage songs and repeat Shakespeare's plays in an admirable manner. He was so well versed in these plays and other writings that he would often answer questions with a quotation.

"At one time the young people of El Reno had a play of some kind. One of the actors became ill and

Mr. George (Booth) filled the place to the great admiration and entertainment of those who saw him. When surprise was expressed at his ability as an actor he replied that he had acted some when he was a young man.

"Regarding his people, he told different stories. One time he said his father was a doctor, and he and a brother were the only children; that his mother had married again and two half brothers were living in the Indian Territory, their name being Smith, and that he had property in the Indian Territory. Again he seemed very lonely at times, and said that he had not a relative in the world. He was subject to fits of melancholia, was extremely sensitive, quick tempered and rather excitable. He said he had never married. There seemed to be something constantly on his mind about which he thought, and which made him miserable. He seemed to love to have one understand that he was in trouble and appreciated sympathy.

"He remained with the Simmons family three months and treated everyone with the greatest kindness and consideration. Never do I remember his mentioning the history of his past life or that he was other than David E. George until the time he thought he was going to die—that was about the middle of April, 1902.

"He had gone up town, but returned shortly and, entering the room where Mrs. Simmons, Mrs. Bears and myself were seated, he made some remarks regarding the weather, which was unusually fine for the time of year. He then went to his room and in about fifteen minutes called for us, and said:

" 'I feel as if I am going to be very sick.' He was lying on his bed and asked me to get him a mirror. For some time he gazed at himself in the mirror.

"Mrs. Bears said she could see the pupils of his eyes dilate and believed that he had taken morphine. Being uneasy, she went out o. the room and got him a cup of coffee and insisted until he drank it, but when she suggested sending for a physician he roused himself and in a peculiar and dramatic manner and voice said, while holding the mirror in front of his face:

" 'Stay, woman, stay. This messenger of death is my guest, and I desire to see the curtain of death fall upon the last tragic act of mine,' which passionate utterance brought tears to our eyes. And when I turned to wipe the tears from my eyes he called me to his side and said:

" 'I have something to tell you. I am going to die in a few minutes, and I don't believe you would do anything to injure me. Did it ever occur to you that I am anything but an ordinary painter? I killed the best man that ever lived.' I asked him who it was and he answered:

" 'Abraham Lincoln.'

"I could not believe it. I thought him out of his head and asked: 'Who was Abraham Lincoln?'

" 'Is it possible you are so ignorant as not to know?' he asked. He then took a pencil and paper and wrote down in a peculiar but legible hand the name, 'Abraham Lincoln,' and said:

" 'Don't doubt it, it is true. I am John Wilkes Booth.'

" 'Am I dying now?' he asked. 'I feel cold, as if death's icy hand was closing my life as the forfeit for my crime.'

"He then told me that he was well off. He seemed to be perfectly rational while talking to me. He knew me and knew where he was, and I believe he really thought in fact that he was dying, and asked me to keep his secret until he was dead, adding that if any one should find out now that he was J. Wilkes Booth they would take him out and hang him, and the people who loved him so well now would despise him. He told me that people high in official life hated Lincoln and were implicated in his assassination. He said that the suspense of possibly being detected preyed on his mind all the time and was something awful, and that his life was miserable. He said that Mrs. Surratt was innocent and he was responsible for her death as well as that of several others. He said that he was devoted to acting, but had to give it up because of his crime, and the fact that he must remain away from the stage, when he loved the life and profession of acting so well, made him restless and ill tempered. He said he had plenty of money, but was compelled to play the character of a working man to keep his mind occupied.

"In the mean time Dr. Arnold arrived and as a result of his efforts Mr. George was restored. After this he was very anxious for weeks regarding what he had told me and questioned me concerning it. I answered him that he had told me nothing of importance, but he seemed to know better. One day he saw me looking at a picture of Lincoln and asked me why I was looking at it. I told him that I had always admired Lincoln.

" 'Is that the only reason you have for looking at it?' he asked, regarding me with a fierce look. A peculiar expression came over his face, his eyes flashed and he turned pale and walked off.

"One peculiar feature of Mr. George, or Booth's, face was that one eyebrow was somewhat higher than the other. I have noticed him limp slightly, but he said it was rheumatism. That Mr. George had a past we all knew, but what his secret was remains unknown except in so far as he may have communicated the truth to me."

Booth's, or George's, life at El Reno was much the same as I have found it at other places—a similarity and accumulative evidence unmistakably establishing his identity of person and character wherever he located. It seems to have been his policy to change his name and character as often as he changed his place of residence. It will be remembered that when he left Hennessy for El Reno that he changed his name from George D. Ryan to David E. George, and his occupation and dress from that of a gentleman of leisure to that of a journeyman painter of houses, which character he acted to such perfection that, although he painted but one house, and did that in such an uneven and unworkmanlike manner as to show that he knew little or nothing about painting, yet people thought he knew all about it, and just why he did no more painting the general public did not understand. Upon inquiry, however, George, or Booth, was always ready with a satisfactory explanation. When the editor of the El Reno Democrat, in which paper he put an advertisement as a tradesman of house painting, at a cost of four dollars a month, thinking it a useless expense, so universally was it known that George, or Booth, did no such work, suggested this to him, George, or Booth, indignantly demanded to know if the editor was uneasy about the price of the card, if so he would pay for it in advance. The editor apologized and the card continued from month to month for two years, up to the date of the death of George.

Booth's purpose in this is obvious. He wanted to keep himself constantly before the public as a painter, not that he wanted work, but to keep alive his identity as a painter while he played the deceptive character. The little cottage painted for Mr. Anstien was the stage setting to the character, the card in the paper was his program and he played to a successful finish this drama of the journeyman painter.

Booth's idea in purchasing the cottage and establishing a home for himself was probably because he thought he would enjoy it after a long and homeless life, alone whether on the plains, in the mountains or the best hotels—for it was his custom to put up at only the best hotels wherever he went. Thus, when he reached El Reno he went to the Anstien Hotel, the best one then in the city, and as good as any there now. But three months of home life was quite sufficient for him and he moved into the Kerfoot Hotel, the newest and most up-to-date hotel in

El Reno, which was completed after he left the Anstien for his cottage. Just how it was possible for Booth to stay at this hotel, the stopping place of most of the traveling public, and escape detection in his changed character from "Gentleman Ryan" to "Journeyman House Painter George," by people from Hennessy, only about sixty-five miles away, who must have frequented this hotel, is hard to understand. Nevertheless it is true. It would be possible, perhaps easy, to deceive as to occupation, but to successfully disguise his person, and change his name, is remarkable and certainly required all the genius of the actor, John Wilkes Booth, who played the change of name, person and character practically in the same community. At El Reno, Guthrie and Enid he was known as George, while at Hennessy, within the same section, he was known as George D. Ryan, and that he was not recognized and exposed staggers comprehension and creates disbelief, nevertheless Booth did this successfully, as he did many other surprising things.

Leaving El Reno, Booth, or George, arrived at Enid on the 3d day of December, 1902, and registered at the Grand Avenue Hotel, under the name of David E. George. In the meantime Mr. Harper and his wife had removed from El Reno to Enid, from which place she made the following statement:

"Enid, Oklahoma Territory, Jan. 23d, 1903.

"On the evening of January 13th, I was startled and surprised by reading in the Enid Daily News of the suicide of David E. George, of El Reno, with whom I first became acquainted in March, 1900, in El Reno, at the home of Mr. Simmons.

"Mr. Harper went down on Wednesday morning, the 14th instant, and recognized him, and told the embalmers of a confession that David E. George had made to myself, and that they had better investigate.

"I went to the morgue with Mr. Harper on the 15th and identified the corpse of David E. George as the man who had confessed to me at El Reno that he was John Wilkes Booth, and, as brevity has been enjoined on me, will reaffirm my former statement made in detail of David E. George's confession to me at El Reno, about the middle of April, 1900, as fully as if same were set forth herein.

(Signed.)   "MRS. E. C. HARPER."

"Territory of Oklahoma,
)ss.
"County of Garland.

"Mrs. E. C. Harper, first being duly sworn, upon her oath says that the facts were written above by herself; that she knows the facts she has written, and that the same are true.

(Signed)   "MRS. E. C. HARPER.

"Sworn to and subscribed before me this the 24th day of January, 1903.

(Signed)   "A. A. STRATFORD,
                              "Notary Public.

(L. S.) "My commission expires November 18th, 1906."

CHAPTER XVI.

PRESS COMMENTS ON THE SUICIDE OF DAVID E. GEORGE.

"Enid Wave: Enid, Oklahoma Territory, January 17th, 1903.—(Special.)—*David E. George, a wealthy resident of the Territory, who committed suicide here, announced himself on his deathbed to be John Wilkes Booth, the assassin of President Lincoln.* He stated that he had successfully eluded the officers after shooting Lincoln and since had remained incognito. His statement caused a sensation, and an investigation was made. Surgeons examined the body and stated the man to be of the age Booth would be at this time, and announced that his leg was broken in the same place and in the same manner as that of Booth after jumping from the President's box at Ford's Theater after the assassination. All the time George has received money regularly from unknown sources, and telegrams arriving yesterday and today ask that the body be held for identification. It is claimed that one telegram came from the address, George E. Smith, Colfax, Iowa, the same as the mysterious money remittances. Smith is unknown to any one in Oklahoma. Upon his arrival in Enid today he commanded that no other person be allowed to view the remains, and promised to return for the body later.

"Mr. Smith was asked if George had ever confessed any of his life's history to him, to which he answered: 'Well, yes, to some extent. He has had a past of which I do not care to speak at the present. I think he killed a man in Texas. He may be Booth.'

"George committed suicide in the Grand Avenue Hotel, taking poison. He previously attempted suicide at El Reno. A letter found in his pocket addressed, 'To Whom It May Concern,' sets aside a former will which he made, although its contents are not known. He was worth about thirty thousand dollars, owning property in El Reno, Oklahoma; in Dallas, Texas, and a lease on six hundred acres in the Indian Territory. He carried $5,000.00 insurance.

"No reason for the suicide is known. George maintained on his death bed to his attendants that he was John Wilkes Booth, and his general appearance closely resembles that of the murderer of Lincoln."

The following appeared in the same paper under proper date:

"Enid, Oklahoma, January 21st, 1903.—The Wave's editorial and reportorial force have been searching closely for data and evidence to sustain or obliterate the report that the remains lying in the Enid morgue, under the name of David E. George, could possibly be those of J. Wilkes Booth, who assassinated Abraham Lincoln nearly thirty-eight years ago. All the history or account of that sad and terrible affair to be found in the city has been searched, and while the history at hand leaves but little doubt of the decease of Booth in attempting to escape from the burning barn in Virginia, that he was shot by Boston Corbett upon his first appearance from the barn, and that he died on the porch of Garrett's Virginia farm home, was taken to Washington, identified and buried secretly, that a

245

diary was found on his person, etc., yet the fact still remains that a doubt did exist with the government as to the positive identity of the man killed; hence the reward for his capture was never paid, for the identity was not clear. The Wave is still of the opinion that the possibility of the dead man being all that is mortal of John Wilkes Booth remains in doubt, but it must be admitted that the evidence goes to show that if George was not Booth he was his double, which, in connection with his voluntary confession to Mrs. Harper, makes the case interesting and worthy the attention of the Attorney General's department of the United States.

Doctors Baker and Way unearthed the December, 1901, number of the Medical Monthly Journal in their office, which number was almost wholly devoted to the consideration of the murderers of the Presidents of the United States and European potentates. In this pamphlet we found a portrait of J. Wilkes Booth, with quite a writeup as to his character, a physical and anatomical description among other descriptions. It said the forehead of J. Wilkes Booth was Kephalonard, the ears excessively and abnormally developed, inclined to the so-called Satanic type; the eyes were small, sunken and unequally placed; the nose was normal; the facial bones and jaw were arrested in development, and there was a partial V-shaped dental arch; the lower jaw was well developed.

"Yesterday the editor of the paper, in company with Dr. McElreth, visited the corpse and compared it with the above description of Booth, and we must acknowledge that the dead man shows all the marks credited to Booth above in every particular. The satanic ear is not much larger than the ordinary ear, but the lower lobe thereof clings close to the side of the head instead of projecting outward like the common or ordinary ear. The corpse has that kind of an ear. The eyebrows of the dead man are not mates in appearance, which fits the description of Booth. The Booth chin, mouth, upper lip and general description is absolutely perfect in the corpse.

"The Wave has been searching for a fac-simile of Booth's handwriting. It was found today in a copy of Harper Brothers' Pictorial History of the Civil

War, and we were startled when we compared it with the round, little, scrawly boy writing of D. E. George. We placed the very last words George wrote by the side of the fac-simile writing of Booth, and it really seemed to us that one and the same man had written both, Booth's fac-simile signature shown in Harper's Pictorial History indicated the same irregular handwriting as George's.

"History readers will remember that a supposed attempt was made to poison President Lincoln in a hotel in Meadeville, Pennsylvania, in August, 1864. A notice appeared in the window of the hotel. saying:

" 'Abe Lincoln departed this life August 1st, 1864, by the effects of poison.'

"After the Washington tragedy this handwriting on the window was found to be the handwriting of J. Wilkes Booth, and as it appeared in Harpers' Pictorial History of the Civil War it is a fac-simile of the writing of D. E. George, now supposed to be Booth."

The Post-Dispatch, of St. Louis, Missouri, through its reportorial staff, made a similar investigation, writing an editorial report in confirmation of the investigation made and published by the Enid Wave as above given, but which is not here reproduced because it would be but cumulative evidence of the subject. However, we do give the following:

"The Perry, Oklahoma Republican: Perry, Oklahoma, June 5th, 1903.—The Booth Case:

"It is now fully developed that the man at Enid, who committed suicide on January 13th last, was none other than John Wilkes Booth, the slayer of President Lincoln. Junius Brutus Booth, the nephew of John Wilkes Booth, has fully identified the picture of David E. George as that of his uncle, John Wilkes Booth.

"It has always been known by the Booth family that John Wilkes Booth was alive, and they have been in constant communication with him ever since April 14th, 1865, the day of President Lincoln's assassination and the escape of John Wilkes Booth. This knowledge on the part of Junius Brutus Booth, the actor, was what prompted him, or his brother Edwin, to make remarks about the supposed grave of J. Wilkes Booth. He or they well knew that the body in the grave was not that of J. Wilkes Booth.

"People conversant with the history of the published capture of Booth, and with the fact that the reward offered by the Federal government for Booth's capture has never been awarded, many always believed him to be alive. From the time of Booth's supposed capture, in April, 1865, until January of this year, J. Wilkes Booth has been in almost constant touch with his friends. Being an actor, and also secluded by the wilds of Texas and Indian Territory, and through the anxious efforts of friends and relatives to preserve his life, it has been an easy matter for Booth to conceal his identity. In this he has been as smooth as was his disguise as an old colored man moving. There are no records, and never have been, in the Federal archives which go to show any positive or direct proof of the death of Booth. There has always been a lingering desire in the hearts of the people to believe that such was the case, but to the close student of affairs a doubt has always existed.

"At the time of the suicide of George in Enid and his claim to be none other than John Wilkes Booth, the Republican stated its belief in the confession of the man. All the facts in the case have pointed, and do now point, to the truthfulness of his death bed statement. For many years George, alias Booth, had been furnished funds by his friends.''

The following is an editorial from the Daily Democrat:

''El Reno, Oklahoma Territory, June 3d, 1903.—

''From the evidence at hand there is no doubt that the man who died at Enid last January, and who was supposed by some to be John Wilkes Booth, the assassin of President Lincoln, was really that man, he having been identified by many who knew John Wilkes Booth before the war, during the war and since that time.

''After the death of the man certain papers found on his person led to the opinion that he was the fugitive assassin supposed to have been killed thirty-three years ago, and the body was embalmed to await a thorough investigation. It has been in an undertaking house here ever since, and all possible efforts have been made to verify the remarkable claim made by the dead man's lawyer, who came from Memphis, Tennessee, and asserted that his client was none other than the slayer of President Lincoln."

The St. Louis Post-Dispatch contained the following:

"St. Louis, Mo., June 3d, 1903.—A special from Enid, Oklahoma, says: 'Junius Brutus Booth, the actor, a nephew of John Wilkes Booth, the assassin of President Lincoln, has fully identified from photographs, etc., the man, David E. George, as his uncle, John Wilkes Booth.

"George, or Booth, committed suicide here January 13th last, and in his effects was found a letter directed to F. L. Bates, Memphis, Tenn., who came here at once and identified the body as that of John Wilkes Booth, and has since secured confirmation of his statement that George is in fact Booth."

The foregoing are a few of the many comments in the various publications made at the time of the suicide confirming the identification of the man known as George to be John Wilkes Booth, showing and reflecting the opinion of the disinterested masses through the expressions of the press, the best and only medium for gathering facts from expression of opinion. I could fill this volume with press reports supporting the identity herein given, and these have merely been used for the secondary purpose of showing how I became advised of the suicide's death.

While I have never been able to secure the letter referred to in the last clipping—it having been taken from the body of the dead man as he lay in the morgue awaiting identification by a mysterious man who claimed to have known George in life, and who disappeared before my arrival on the scene—still it was seen by two gentlemen of integrity and served the direct purpose of additional confirmation of the identity of the body as that of Booth. I presume that this letter was the basis of the telegram received by me about the 17th of January, 1903, asking me to come to Enid and identify the body of John Wilkes Booth. In answer to this telegram I left Memphis that same afternoon for Enid.

Owing to many washouts over the Frisco System, which line I took to Enid, I was several days reaching the latter point. I missed connection at El Reno on account of these delays, where transfers are made

for Enid, and had to remain there one night. I
wired the clerk of the Grand Avenue Hotel, however, that I would reach there the next morning. I
was met at the Enid depot by Mr. Brown, the clerk
of the hotel named, who informed me that my coming was awaited with great anxiety by a large and
much-excited throng of people from widely located
sections of the country, and that there was a large
number of old Federal soldiers in the city, who, it
had been whispered about, intended to take the body
into the streets and burn it, if it should be identified
as that of John Wilkes Booth. He suggested that I
register under an assumed name, and that I should
play the role of a drummer for a furniture house,
carrying as a specialty feather top mattresses, saying that as T. B. Road was the password for Booth
at the Potomac bridge, so feather top mattresses was
to be the password which would make me known to
Mr. Pennaman, who was a large furniture dealer as
well as proprietor of the undertaking establishment
and morgue of the city where the body of Booth lay
in state. It was estimated that more than fifty
thousand men, women and children had viewed the

body of Booth. The crowd had grown so great that the doors to the morgue had to be closed, as it seemed that the place would be actually picked to pieces by the souvenir hunters; they had cut up the carpets, rugs, curtains, shades, furniture and everything else in the house convenient at the time.

We had plenty of time to talk on the way from the depot to the Grand Avenue Hotel, as it seems a part of the plan in the West to locate the depots as far from the town and hotels as possible, to add as much inconvenience and expense as the traveling public can stand, I suppose. Arriving at the hotel we found a large crowd of excited men in earnest conversation, but scanning every passenger who entered the hotel. I walked up to the desk and registered as Charles O'Connor, of New York City. As I turned away from the register a tall, well-dressed young man glanced at the name and I could not help a quiet smile at his disgust when he read the name I had just written. And I smile even now when I recall the tall, dark, olive-complected, black-eyed reporter, who expressed such contempt in his manner as he glanced at the insignificant man with so ex-

alted a name. He was on a hot trail, but so far away.
If he is living now I hope he will read this story and
learn how well he judged his man, and that I now
forgive him.

After being dusted off and otherwise perfecting
my toilet, I walked into the spacious breakfast room
of the hotel, where I was again met by Mr. Brown,
who joined me at a private table specially prepared
and removed from the other guests in the room.

By this time I was well on to my job—necessity
being the mother of invention—I had early made my
plans, and said to Mr. Brown, in the most familiar
way:

"Well, Brown, how did you like that last furniture shipped you by my house? We had to ship the
feather mattresses out from Cincinnati, not having
them in stock in New York, and hope they proved
entirely satisfactory. We are anxious to maintain
our already established reputation in the West for
correct dealing. Especially do I hope those light
walnut suites, which I personally inspected before
shipment, were satisfactory, and that no fault could
be found with them, as they were of patterns a spe-

cialty by our leading designers.'' Then in an undertone I asked Brown if the word "designers" was the correct thing in this connection.

"D—— if I know," he replied in a whisper. Then in a pleasant, natural tone of voice, audible to those present, he said: "The shipment made us by your house, as a whole, has been entirely satisfactory, and the feather top mattresses were by far the best of their kind in the market. By the way, W. B. Pennaman wants to carry those mattresses in this market, and it would be well for you to see him."

"Thank you very much for this information, and since I don't know his location in the city I shall trouble you for directions as to how to find him. I shall certainly call on him the very first thing.

"By the way, Brown, what is the meaning of all this excitement in town? Is there a widely advertised circus or an election going on?" I asked, turning to him, showing surprise in both voice and manner.

"No," he said, "it is on account of the suicide at this hotel the other day of a man who is supposed to be John Wilkes Booth."

"Yes, I have read something of that in the newspapers during the past few days," I said, "but did not suppose a report of this character would create the present state of excitement. But, from what I read in the newspapers, I thought Booth killed himself at El Reno."

"No, Booth lived at El Reno, but killed himself in this place, Enid."

"Is this all a farce?" I asked, but at this juncture Mr. Brown was called to the office and I finished my breakfast in silence and alone.

Gaining the information as to the location of Pennaman's place of business, I at once went to the store of the undertaker and furniture dealer. On entering the store I saw a number of clerks, all busy. At the center desk was a handsome man of thirty-five or forty; but which of these men was Pennaman, to whom I was to talk feather top mattresses, was my proposition. I sized up the men, walked over to the center desk, introduced myself as Charles O'Connor and inquired for Mr. Pennaman. The gentleman before me acknowledged himself to be the man inquired for, and I told him that I was representing one of the largest furniture houses in the East; that we made a specialty of feather top mattresses, and I would be glad to make a date with him to present the merits of the line of goods carried by my firm, and invited him to call on me at the commercial parlors of the Grand Avenue Hotel at any hour convenient to him, where I would take pleasure in presenting samples and prices, which I thought would prove attractive. He told me he was then quite busy, but asked that I be seated, and unlatching the gate to the railing around his desk, he invited me inside and pointed to the papers on the table. This done, he excused himself and with a polite indifference to my presence proceeded with his letter writing.

As a matter of fact, this table and chair had been placed there for me in anticipation of my coming. The papers were those containing the news of Booth's suicide, etcetera, as well as photographs taken of Booth after death. I could only admire this delicate way of furnishing me, unobserved, the means of identifying the body of Booth without actually seeing it, if it should not be opportune to do so. The recognition of St. Helen, or Booth, in the pictures provided was instantaneous.

On the back of the pictures was written in a small, fine hand with a pencil: "Conceal and take these pictures with you and call my attention when you desire. I am busy, you know, and must not be annoyed by you."

Having finished my inspection, I turned to him and said: "Well, Mr. Pennaman, how are you off for feather top mattresses?"

"I have none in stock," he replied, rising and leading the way out.

That I might be identified as a drummer for a furniture house we continued our conversation for the edification of others as we passed through the store, discussing classes, prices, grades of mattresses and furnitures, we walked back to a side entrance, commanding a view of the street on which the morgue fronted. Seeing the way clear—no people having collected there—we passed back through the store, where Mr. Pennaman introduced me to the man in charge of the morgue and the body of Booth as Charles O'Connor, a drummer for a furniture house. This gentleman led us through a back way to the morgue, which we entered from a rear door into the front room, where lay the body of John .Wilkes Booth, the man who had been called by the people in this community David E. George. In the presence of the attendant and Mr. Pennaman, cold, stiff and dead, I beheld the body of my friend, John St. Helen. After a separation of more than twenty-six years I knew him as instantly as men discern night from day, as the starlight from moonlight, or the moon from the light of day.

You ask what did I say? I don't know. Mr. Pennaman says I exclaimed, "My God! St. Helen, is it possible?" Then my manhood softened into sentiment and soul into tears. Spread the veil of charity upon the deeds of the dead, that mantle of death cast in the loom of sorrow and woven in the warp and woof of sighs and tears. Shaken with emotion for my dead friend, I had no thought of the crime that this man had committed while his body lay at rest, seeming to sleep in pleasant repose.

In a few minutes I recovered. I realized now for the first time that I was in the presence of John

Wilkes Booth, though I had, in fact, been told so more than a quarter of a century before. I had the tintype picture which St. Helen had given me at Granberry, Texas, twenty-six years ago. I took it out and called upon Pennaman and the attendant to bear witness with me to the identity of this dead man with the picture, which I showed them, when they replied without a moment's hesitation:

"We need no picture to identify this man in your presence. Yes, this is the same man. It is an axiomatic fact, not debatable, they are one and the same man."

We then compared the high thumb joint on the right hand, the small scar in the right brow—the uneven brow—the scar received in the accident mentioned by Miss Clara Morris, raises this brow to an uneven line with the left; the right leg was examined and we found a slight indentation on the surface of the shin bone—Booth's leg was not literally broken, there was a fracture of the shin bone six inches above the ankle; I should say a split or slight shivering of the bone, for besides the identation on the front of the shin bone there were small scars plainly discernable, where particles of bone seemed to have worked out through the skin (St. Helen, Booth, told me this himself), leaving small round scars, while the general shape of the leg at this point seemed curved a little. His eyes, head, forehead, chin, mustache and hair were all the same as John St. Helen's, and compared exactly with the picture of St. Helen, taken at the time before stated, and given to me, the only difference being that the hair and mustache were streaked with gray now, especially the mustache, which was quite gray at its parting, under the nose. His complexion, even in death, retained somewhat its characteristic olive tint, and his beautiful neck and shoulders were yet preserved. His weight was about one hundred and sixty pounds, height about five feet, eight or nine inches. His shoulders were square, while his neck rose from his chest and shoulders as beautifully as the most beautifully formed woman's, masculine it is true, but with that beautiful symmetry of form. The embalmer called my attention to this fact, saying that when he began the operation of embalming the body he thought it advisable to make an incision at the point where the throat enters the chest, just above the breastbone, and showed me a slight abrasion there, but noticing this beautiful formation of the body, he let it remain intact, regarding it as a formation of art too beautiful to destroy, even in a dead body.

Lest my presence might be discovered, we left the morgue, and not a word was spoken until we reached Mr. Pennaman's desk. He was almost in a state of collapse. He held out his hand, I clasped it, it was cold and clammy, as the hand of the dead; he was pale to pallor, and told me that he had never undergone such a mental and physical experience. He explained to me that he had formerly been connected with the New York Sun, was one of the city editors of that paper; that he had written up John Wilkes Booth in detail, supposing him dead, and that now, after all these years, that Booth's dead body should fall into his hands was truly and unmistakably a shock to him. Even the veteran embalmer looked pale and worn, and as he stood leaning against Mr. Pennaman's desk he remarked, "This is the experience of my life."

I returned to the Grand Avenue Hotel, passing on my way crowds of men standing here and there in earnest conversation, with serious faces and determined manner. While walking through these groups of men I imagine I had the feeling possessed by the man who, robed in a red blanket, passes in the presence of a mad bull in the Mexican amphitheater. Nevertheless I must go, and I went with the full determination to say feather mattresses and all kinds of furniture talk to the first fellow who looked ugly and angry at me; however, my knowledge of Western customs and Western habits stood me in good stead now. I knew who to trust, and he was there in large force. With mimic snakes around his hat, spurs on his boots, goat skins on his legs and quirt in his hand he was there, and he was my friend— one on whom I could depend—the Cow Boy.

You ask, did I belong to the Cow Boy Union? There is no such thing that I have ever heard of. No. The fact is, one Cow Boy is often the whole thing by himself.

What would I say to him? Well, I would not have said feather top mattresses to him, as I did to Pen-

naman or   hers.   But in good Western style I
would have said, if pursued by an angry mob: ''Mill
'em, boys. Mill 'em. Round 'em up. Keep your
eye on the lead steer.'' This is meaningless to you,
but to the cow boy it would have been an introduction, as a cow boy, and to be a cow boy among cow
boys is a thing to be appreciated in times of personal danger.

However, with a manner that indicated indifference to surrounding dangers, I wended my way to
the hotel, where Mr. Brown gave me the inside facts
about Booth's, or George's, coming to the hotel. He
said:

''The press reports about George's coming to the
Grand Avenue Hotel and registering on the morning
of the 3d day of December, 1902, are correct. While
here George was a constant reader of newspapers, remaining in the reading room and office most of the
time. He seemed to be a man of perfect leisure,
paid his bills by the week promptly, was genial and
pleasant in his manner, had a tendency to drink a
little too much at times and remained up late at
nights, but was a reasonably early riser. When I

was on night watch he was great company to me; he was well read, often repeating parts of Shakespeare's plays and reciting other poetry, which it seemed natural to him to know, reciting it in such a manner as to be highly entertaining.

"At times George would become sad or rather thoughtfully silent. In these moods his discussion would drift to matters of the 'hereafter.' I asked him, 'You mean after death?' He replied, 'Yes.'

"I remember one night we were alone; he was in what I called his 'off' mood. He raised himself erect in his chair, and in a tragic manner, with gestures and expression suited to the words, he said:

" 'Am I better than the dog? Oh, no. He is far better than I! He is capable of no sin or crime. Yet when he is found dead his body is placed in the garbage box. Then why not ship my body without a crate to the potters field of the dog? But I, even I, a man, am unworthy that the putrid flesh shall be torn from my bones by the vultures that pray upon the flesh of the dead brute.'

"These utterances were made with such strong self-accusation that I wondered what it could mean, and from that time on I watched every move of the man and listened attentively to every word he said. Whether it was what George said or the manner in which he said a thing, I can't quite understand, but what he said always impressed you. Of this I am sure, in all my twenty years experience in the hotel business I have never seen such another character.

"He was a handsome man for his age. His black eyes, when in repose, seemed to have lost luster by age, but in conversation or when repeating verses from Shakespeare, or other recitations, they would kindle, flash and sparkle as if inspired or ignited into flame from the burning souls of the eternally damned, while his shapely face and magnificent forehead paled rather from his natural olive. Sitting or standing with a natural, easy grace, in such moods be made a picture one felt privileged to behold, and never to be forgotten. To my dying day the meeting of this man George, or Booth, will be remembered by me as an epoch in my life.

"It is true, Bates. Be this man who he may, George, Ryan, Marr, St. Helen, Smith or Booth, he is a man without a model. He looks like no one else, he acted like no one else and he talked like no one else that I ever knew or saw."

"Well, Brown, who is this man?"

"I believe him to be John Wilkes Booth, as he stated on his dying bed. In fact, I don't think he could be any one else."

"Did he at any time before his death intimate his identity other than George?"

"No, he did not. In his manner he was quite unobtrusive and mixed but little with the people in the hotel, and the scenes and recitations I have referred to would always be at a time when we were alone, and the people in the hotel supposed to be asleep."

"I noticed that some of the press reports state that George committed suicide in the morning."

"This was not the case. On the night of the 13th of January, 1903, George came into the office and reading room as usual and spent some time reading and finally writing letters. When he had finished the letters, about ten o'clock p. m., he said he was going down to the drug store, just half a block up the street. He was gone only a short time, when he

269

came to the desk, obtained the key to his room and bade me goodnight, requesting to be called for breakfast if he should oversleep his usual time. I saw or heard nothing more of him until about half past eleven o'clock, when I heard groans coming from the first floor just above the office, in the direction of the room occupied by George. The watchman came in hurriedly and we went at once to his room. On forcing his door we found him writhing and groaning in great pain. A doctor was called, he pronounced the patient suffering from the effects of poison and began vigorous treatment at once. The pains seemed to come and go, and George seemed to be suffering the greatest agony. After awhile I noticed that the pains or spasms seemed to come closer together, and the patient was drifting from under the control or force of the antidotes, and witnessed the most horrifying struggle for life I ever saw or ever could imagine. About four o'clock in the morning the doctor lost all hope of saving his patient, and informed George that if he had anything to arrange he had better do so. In the meantime Mr. Dumont, the proprietor of the hotel, had come into the room, the doctor having left. George said:

" 'I have only to say, my name is not George. I am John Wilkes Booth, and I request that my body be sent to the morgue for identification,' when death came and relieved the suffering of the man whose name we did not then know, and he died at 6:20 o'clock on the morning of January 14th, 1903.

"The undertaker was notified and George's body removed to the morgue, as he had requested. When it became generally reported that the man's true name was John Wilkes Booth neither Mr. Dumont or myself had ever seen Mr. Booth nor any member of his family and consequently could not affirm or deny the fact of the true identity of the man, though I was ready to believe then, and do now believe, that George, the man who died, is, in fact, John Wilkes Booth, as he said. The truth is I would believe anything he said, and I understand that he confessed his true identity to a Mrs. Harper of this city, who has identified the body as that of Booth."

STATEMENT OF MESSRS. DUMONT and BROWN
"Enid, Oklahoma Territory, Jan. 21st, 1903.

"To Whom It May Concern: We, S. S. Dumont, proprietor, and B. B. Brown, clerk, of the Grand Avenue Hotel, in the city of Enid, and Territory of Oklahoma, declare that we, and each of us, knew a gentleman who registered as a guest of said hotel on the 3d day of December, 1902, under the name of D. E. George, who on the 13th day of January, 1903, committed suicide in said hotel by taking fif teen grains of strychnine or arsenic, and died from the effects of said poison at 6:30 o'clock a. m., on the 14th day of January, 1903, and that we have this day been shown by F. L. Bates, of Memphis, Tennessee, a small tintype picture, together with a photograph, and we say that said tintype picture and photograph are the same and perfect pictures or likenesses in each and every feature of the said D. E. George, the only difference being that George, or whomsoever he was, was older at the time of his death than when the pictures were taken.

(Signed)   "B. B. BROWN.

                               S. S. DUMONT.

"Sworn to and subscribed before me this, the 22d day of January, 1903.

    (Signed)   "GUY S. MANOTT,

    (L. S.)   "Notary Public.

"My commission expires October 22d, 1906."

CHAPTER XVII.

THESE ARE PICTURES OF JOHN WILKES BOOTH.

At the conclusion of my interview with Messrs. Dumont and Brown I left the confinement of the hotel for the fresh air and scenes of the street. It was about four o'clock in the afternoon, the streets were thronged with people, as they had been in the morning, while men, women and children were hurrying to and fro on the sidewalks. But the crowds seemed to have in a measure left the public square, where the whole surface of the earth had been worn perfectly smooth by the press of human feet. In the rear, to the north and west of the little city of Enid, could be seen many camps and covered wagons, near which staked and hobbled horses browsed on the outlying commons. Small camp fires burned slowly and watch dogs lay silent on the camp grounds, near or under the front wheels of the wagons, keeping guard while the master, mistress and the children walked the streets of Enid or stood in groups around the camp grounds. Everywhere was that expression of hard, intense feeling that I had never seen before at any time, and never expect to see again. Why was this? It was said that the body of the man who had assassinated President Lincoln lay in the morgue in Enid. It was expected that this body would be identified by a man who should have arrived in the morning. If the body was pronounced to be that of John Wilkes Booth it was planned to make a great bonfire and burn it in the public streets of Enid. Yes, the body was to be tied to a shaft and burned while surrounded by men, women and children, hooting, shouting and chanting triupmhant songs of revenge for the death of President Lincoln. And when the savage deed was done the flickering flames from the burning body of the assassin would have lighted the pathway of the avengers as they homeward trod.

And I, the man expected and looked for with such anxiety, walked among them, and they knew it not. I stood there, not in fear, not in awe, but in bewildered horror as imagination conjured up before me the contemplated scene. And as I gazed about me at these people I asked myself: What manner of man was Abraham Lincoln that his memory should be thus entombed in the hearts of these people, so far removed from him and the scenes of his life and death—many of whom, in fact, were born long years after he had died? How wonderful was this strange appreciation of the man. It was a lesson to me, a living proof of the truth that "the good men do live after them." About me were men and women bowed with age, shaking with palsied limbs, earnest men and women in middle life, ordinarily busied with its duties and demands, and bright youth, girls and boys, flushed with its dreams and hopes, and tender children, all treading the paths and streets which led from camp and home to the threshold of the morgue, where lay the supposed body of John Wilkes Booth, silent in self-inflicted death, his own hand avenging the crime it had committed.

Strange, indeed, was this spectacle! I moved here and there among them, watching, wondering, my heart beating in unison with the hearts of the strange human concourse about me, until twilight came and

JOHN WILKES BOOTH, AGED 64.
(11 Days After Death.) In the Morgue at Enid, Much Swollen From the Poison He Had Taken.

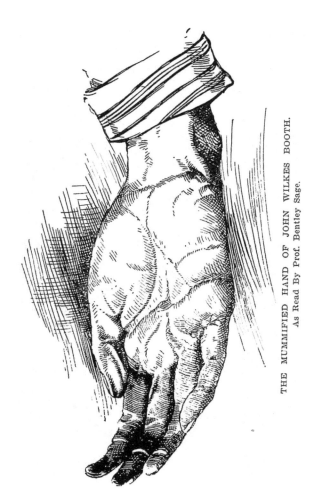

THE MUMMIFIED HAND OF JOHN WILKES BOOTH.
As Read By Prof. Bentley Sage.

the darkness was starred by electricity as the current reached the arcs that light this beautiful city. Then I turned and walked back to the hotel, acknowledging the pleasant greeting of Mr. Brown as I entered the dining room.

Shortly after dinner Mr. Pennaman called for a consultation with respect to the disposition of the body of Booth. The first conclusion reached was to perfectly preserve the body, if it could be done, which was much doubted by the embalmer, Mr. Ryan, though he promised that his best efforts would be put forth to this end. The only defect at that time existing was a small black splotch on the right cheek just under the eye, which was puzzling the undertaker, who said it might be due to coagulated blood, which would be a bad sign; then, again, the same condition might be brought about by the large amount of poison taken, which might or might not be conducive to the preservation of the body.

This question being settled, the second proposition was likewise disposed of by Mr. Pennaman, at my suggestion agreeing to take out letters of administration on the estate of the dead man, which would include the body, and this he did. Mr. Ryan immediately left us to begin his efforts at absolute preservation of the body.

Mr. Pennaman remained with me, going to the depot and saying good-bye. For, my mission being now completed, I paid the bill of Charles O'Connor of New York and took the 'bus for the depot. On arriving at the depot we found the train would be on time, in fact, over the undulating prairie the beacon light of the engine could be seen rising like a star above the horizon; it grew larger and larger, then rushed onward until the ponderous engine and heavy train slowed down to stop at the station. Unlike the Arab, I did not fold my tent and quietly steal away, but boldly took the southbound cannon ball of the Rock Island. On this train there was much discussion of the tragic affair at Enid; every passenger had his or her own theory as to the suicide and proper identity of David E. George, while some wise men asserted that it was all a fake on the part of the citizens of Enid to advertise that little town and let the world know there was such a place. These and kindred expressions were heard on all sides. There was an old man on the car who had evidently belonged to the Federal army, for I overheard him saying something about belonging to post so-and-so of the G. A. R.'s, a man who had distinguished himself, in my mind, for having more brains and less tongue than the majority of the others. He said: "Well, boys, if the man who killed himself at Enid is Booth, he has not yet been so identified, and it's reported that he left considerable of an estate, and judging others by myself, I would say, if he had been a dear, misguided dead relative of mine, with an estate of thirty or forty thousand dollars, I surely would have looked him up and been chief mourner, and shed tears like our crocodiles on a sandbar in the sunlight of an August midday on a Southern beach. My sorrow would have found vent like unto the sound of foghorns at sea. Then, too, I would not have been particular as to the character or appearance of my very dear relative, the main point being was he dead, very dead; did he have the property and was it mine. Then, too, I understand that this man confessed to his identity as John Wilkes Booth, and that he has never been identified as David E. George, therefore he must be John Wilkes Booth, for in God's name what had this man to gain by such a confession? Could it add to his pleasures, or could it profit the dead? And since by his own hand he died, notoriety could not have been his purpose. No. For what good does notoriety do the dead? No, as to me, I had rather be a living private than a dead general."

What this old man said put me to thinking, looking for the motive a man could have in taking his own life and the confession of a crime on his dying bed which he did not commit, which could only bring upon him the contempt and condemnation of all men. On the other hand, if this man had been George, the fake, it would have been his glory to have impersonated Booth while he lived, to have masqueraded as a notorious murderer, that he might have enjoyed while he lived a character akin to the village bully, the red-eyed-gentleman-from-Bitter-Creek style, a personal character usually as cowardly as it is contemptible. And today I find no reason so satisfactory to nature as that Booth, burdened with the crime he had committed, conscience-whipped and at bay, ended his life by his own hand, willing that his taking away should be deliberate, that he should yet have time and opportunity to confess his crime; for I can conceive the horror of men who die without the opportunity to confess, for remember we have prayed from our infancy up, ''Deliver us from sudden death.''

The man who commits suicide does so from a motive, for a purpose, being insane does not change the purpose, the motive, death preferred, superinduced by sorrow of heart or insanity of mind or a desire to die as a punishment to one's self, or in reparation of our wrongs to others.

Who can so well take his own life as the man who takes the life of another by assassination? It is the man of deliberation who assassinates. It is the man of deliberation who suicides. The acts are kindred of purpose—the immediate taking of life by violence, premeditated and deliberate as a wicked and depraved purpose, or for a wrong, imaginary or real, by the assassin.

In truth it can be said that the man who sheds
blood with the assassin's hand, by his own hand his
own blood, will most likely be shed.

While on our train plunged as if mad with fright,
the engine with her five-foot driving wheels meas-
ured the length of her burden over tracks of steel
on time that must soon land us at El Reno. Then
I felt the pulsation of lessening momentum, I heard
the signal cry of the air brakes, the touch of assuming power and the echo of the wings of the wind as
they wound us within their folds, when motionless
we stood, while the engine was throbbing with its
pent-up power and hissing from its cylinder heads
as if angered at this intrusion and delay. I looked
and we were at El Reno, in the midnight hours. Then
I was off for the Kerfoot Hotel, for a few hours of
rest.

I retired with orders to be called for a ten o'clock
breakfast. Going upstairs, I found that by incident
I had been given room sixty-four, the very one occupied by George, or Booth, the greater part of the
past two years, during his residence at El Reno, he
having left this very room for Enid just forty-one

days before his suicide. Retiring, tired, restless, worried, yet rewarded, I pillowed my head with its feverish brain to enter the land of sleep, an exile from the cares of life.

Rap, rap, rap sounded on the door, and I was awake. The night was gone and the morrow had begun. First to breakfast and then on the street I looked with interest on each thing because it was to me a city new and strange. Then, too, an additional interest was lent because it was the last known home of John Wilkes Booth, the murderer, the assassin of President Lincoln. I looked with wonder and astonishment at the evidence of wealth, civilization and refinement around me. I passed the banks with their hoarded wealth. I passed the merchants who held their wares behind plate glass fronts. I passed the homes of the press, from which were issued the daily papers. I looked upward to see the towering churches and cathedrals with spires which point to the dial of heaven, builded by the hands of reverent men.

El Reno then can not be the home of soulless people, of murderers and assassins alone, for I met and intermingled with its people, its bankers, its merchants, its editors and its ministers, and all I found to be just, honorable and God-fearing people, who spurned, as you do, the murderer, and would punish as you would the assassin. Men who would turn pale and women become agitated at the realization that they, in fact, had known and associated with John Wilkes Booth for more than two years without ever knowing his identity.

I shall never forget my meeting with Mr. Grant, then the proprietor, publisher and editor of the Republican, a daily paper of El Reno, who when I called on him, requested to see my pictures of John Wilkes Booth, and who recognized them to be likenesses of David E. George. When told that George was, in fact, John Wilkes Booth, Mr. Grant expressed great astonishment and indignation at the idea that George could possibly have been John Wilkes Booth. Finally, putting his head forward for a moment, as if in thought, he said: "I tell you what I will do. If you will go with me to the El Reno State Bank and show these pictures to Mr. Bellamy, one of the officers of that bank, and when you show the pictures to him don't say who they are, and if he recognizes them, as I have done, as being true likenesses of David E. George, then I am ready to admit that John Wilkes Booth, the assassin of President Lincoln, has been a citizen of our town in the person of David E. George.''

His proposition was accepted, and over to the bank we went, some few blocks away. Walking to the desk of Mr. Bellamy, I was properly introduced and handed him the tintype picture which St. Helen had left with me in Texas, as well as the photographs which had been taken for the identification of D. E. George as Booth. On handing the pictures to Mr. Bellamy I asked him, ''Who is this man in the picture?'' Without hesitation he replied, ''Why, this is David E. George in his younger days.'' Then followed the recognition of the pictures as those of David E. George by the other officers and employes of this and other banks, as has been heretofore mentioned.

Mr. Grant accepted the situation and said, with some emotion, ''I shall write this matter up fully in my paper tomorrow morning.'' Whether the publication was ever made I am not advised.

I next found myself with Mr. Hennley, owner, editor and publisher of the Daily Democrat, of El Reno, who had known David E. George well, and readily identified him from the pictures which I have just mentioned as having been identified by Mr. Grant, Mr. Bellamy and others.

The city editor of the Democrat, a gentleman whose name I believe was Brown, and who had removed to El Reno from some Western city a short time before to enter the employment of Mr. Hennley, became interested in our conversation and was handed the pictures by Mr. Hennley. He instantly said:

''I never saw David E. George, and I know nothing of him, but these are the pictures of John Wilkes Booth.''

''Did you know John Wilkes Booth personally?'' I asked him.

''I did, and I knew him well, personally and on the stage. I regarded him as the greatest actor of his day on the American stage, and never missed an opportunity to see him. I saw him and heard him in Baltimore and New York often, and in Washington also, where I was connected with the Federal army, and saw him on the streets, frequently meeting him and speaking with him as a personal acquaintance. I remember that I saw him for the last time on the street only a short time before the assassination. I also know other members of the Booth family and could not be mistaken about this picture.

"I was in Washington City at the time of the assassination and later, when the body of the man claimed to be Booth was brought there, and owing to the secrecy and the mysterious manner of handling that body after it reached Washington there was a belief, quite general among the members of the Federal army with whom I came in contact, that the body held was not that of John Wilkes Booth. These recent developments in the discovery and identification of John Wilkes Booth have been no surprise to me."

I next went to the Anstien Hotel and met the proprietors of this house, where David E. George first put up on moving to El Reno. On showing the pictures to them they at once identified them in the following authentic manner:

"El Reno, Oklahoma Territory, Jan. 23d, 1903.

"To Whom it May Concern: We, N. J. Anstien and G. F. Anstien, proprietors of the Anstien Hotel, situated in the city of El Reno, after examination of the tintype picture and photographs shown us by F. L. Bates, of Memphis, Tenn., say that the same are true and correct pictures of one D. E. George, or a man who claimed to be of that name. This man, George, boarded at this hotel for a long time. We knew him well, and do not hesitate to pronounce the pictures shown us to be those of this man, and we fully corroborate the statements of Messrs. Dumont and Brown, as fully as if incorporated in this statement.

(Signed.)   "N. J. ANSTIEN.
                          "G. F. ANSTIEN.

"Sworn to and subscribed before me this, the 23d day of January, 1903.

(Signed.)   "FRANK MEYER.
(L. S.)   "Notary Public.

"My commission expires 6-12-05."

THESE ARE PICTURES OF JOHN WILKES BOOTH.

The Messrs. Anstien said: "It was plain to be seen that the man who called himself George was not a painter; that, in fact, he did not know how to properly mix paints or to spread it after it was mixed, but his taste was good, his idea of the arrangement of colors with respect to blending them into harmony was splendid, and as a paint talker he was a success, but as a practical labor painter he was a dismal failure. We supposed this to be the reason why he did not work at what he claimed to be his trade. Then there was the further fact that he always had plenty of money and was prompt at the payment of his bills, whether he worked or did not work, which made it a matter that, in fact, did not concern others.

"When George, or Booth, bought the cottage for thirty-five hundred dollars he lacked a small amount of having enough money to pay cash for it. He came to the office and requested this amount as a loan for a few days. The money was handed him without a question or a note, and promptly on the day agreed upon for its return he came in and paid the money. Where it came from was a mystery, but that did not concern us, so long as he kept his word. And during the long time that he boarded at this hotel he met all his bills with equal promptness and satisfaction. He was regarded as the soul of honor by those with whom he came in contact, personally or in a business way, and while he was queer, or what we would commonly call cranky,'' and as the elder man said, "always spouting poetry, everybody liked him. I told him that he knew much more about Shakespeare and other books than he did about painting and paint brushes.

" 'If you (Mr. Anstien) could spread and display it in certain places as well as I can you would not need to keep a hotel,' Booth had replied on one of these occasions. (Do you catch his meaning—to spread and display paint on the actor?)

The elder Anstien says that "after these little unpleasant sallies," Booth seemed to take a dislike to him, which was regarded as the principal reason for his changing his boarding place.

The cottage which Booth bought was sold by him about a year before he committed suicide, after he went to the Kerfoot Hotel.

THESE ARE PICTURES OF JOHN WILKES BOOTH.

There is one fact that has struck me with great force respecting the identification of Booth, and that is, he affected the same style of dress during his entire life. It will be noticed that his dress at twenty-seven, thirty-eight and sixty-four are practically the same. He always wore a black semi-dress suit style, of the best fabrics, always with the turndown Byron collar and dark tie. His dress at the time he committed suicide was of the same character, his suit being tailormade, new and well pressed, his pants well creased, his shoes new patent leather and his hat a new black Stetson derby. This style of dress, it seems, being a physical characteristic of John Wilkes Booth.

CHAPTER XVIII.

READING THE PALM OF JOHN WILKES BOOTH.

After remaining in El Reno about forty-eight hours, having completed my investigation of Booth's identity, I returned to my home in Memphis, Tennessee, without further incident. Scarcely had I reached home, however, when I was recalled to Enid by the administrator of Booth's estate. On my return I found public sentiment in Enid much quieted down and it was no longer necessary for me to impersonate the character of another. I found that two men supposed to be in the secret service of the United States government—which fact they did not deny—had requested and been permitted to view the body of Booth. They were provided with pictures of John Wilkes Booth, which they compared with Booth's body, and having satisfied themselves that the body was that of Booth, they appealed to the Territorial legal authorities to compel the burial of the body, without denying at any time that the body was that of John Wilkes Booth. But before I reached Enid the matter had been satisfactorily arranged, in what way I did not at that time learn, and I found the body unburied and in a state of perfect preservation, still being held for further identification, challenging, as it were, those in authority, or those of contrary opinion, to show that this body was not that of John Wilkes Booth.

During this visit I learned that Mr. L. Treadkell, who had employed Booth as a teamster, as heretofore mentioned, was then living within nine miles of the city. I at once communicated with him and he came in. On being shown the tintype picture of St. Helen, so often referred to, he readily identified it as the picture of Jesse Smith, his teamster in the early part of the year 1867. He also identified the picture of Booth at the ages of twenty-seven, thirty-eight and sixty-four as being pictures taken from one and the same man, the only difference being the matter of age.

During this visit Bentley Sage, the well known palmist, made the trip to Enid for the express purpose of examining the palms of the now notorious character, whose body lay in the morgue at Enid, known as George, and identified as John Wilkes Booth. The reading follows:

"I discover this hand to be of the spatulate type, from which I learn that the subject was emotional, erratic and governed almost entirely by inspiration. Persons who have this hand are controlled by impulse and are carried to extremes by the impressions of the instant. They are what science might term impractical. Of bright purpose and brilliant promise, they almost invariably fail to materialize their ideas. They are etherial and poetic. Their hopes are rarely fulfilled and they are not only a disappointment to themselves, but they disappoint their friends by their failure to accomplish the real and material things of useful and practical life.

"This subject was no exception. His intellect was keen and wide awake and took in the details and peculiarities of everything he saw, but he lacked the faculty of applying his mind toward the execution of his ideas. Like all those of a spatulate type, his vivid reason was the admiration of his associates, because of his effervescent enthusiasm and optimism, but he never came down to earth from the heights of imagination, and remained pleasure-loving, jovial and incomprehensible, was subject to moods of melancholy and morbidness. These latter characteristics, however, belong to those of the spatulate type. It is the non-fruition of hope to which this moodiness is due in the spatulate hand. It is the sensitive hand that is easily repulsed, especially is this true of this individual hand. He was repelled by a gross nature, but still he had a large faculty for friendship and a strong desire for intellectual and genial companionship.

"Let it be understood that the foregoing is a study of the whole hand, which, owing to its peculiar class, being that of the spatulate, is weak in many respects. In order to correctly understand throughout the balance of this disquisition it will be necessary to take the hand in subdivisions and describe each division.

"I will begin with the thumb, which is of unusual length. All thumbs show the possession of or lack of leadership, will power, control, integrity, reasoning, planning, logic and stability.

"In this thumb I find a man of unbending nature, one who is set in his opinions and ideas, and one whom facts impress strongly, but who did not analyze them carefully, generally depending on observation and the acts of others. At the base of the thumb is the mount of Venus—Venus was the mother of Love—Venus indicates the desires of life acting upon the line of heart. His mount being full and broad at the base, indicates the emotional and sentimental. The mount of Jupiter at the base of the index finger shows pride, ambition and self-esteem. This man had great ambition and great aspirations. He was sensitive to a fault, and the crosses and triangles found upon this mount indicate that his ambitions were never realized. His life was materially affected by disappointments and hopes that were never realized. At the base of the second finger is the mount of Saturn, which indicates the talents and gifts of the individual. His would have been literature, music, art and imitating. Being full of inspiration he could have developed the talents of art and imitating which, together with an entertaining disposition and gestures that were smooth and appropriate, he possessed the faculty of making every movement pleasant to those in his society. He was a man of elegance and charm.

"The mount of Apollo, located at the base of the ring finger, indicates the success of past, present and future, and in this particular case I find the mount to be undeveloped, showing that he had not reached the height of his ambitions, and showing that he had lived under many heavy strains, due to past failures and excitements.

"The mount of Mercury at the base of the little finger indicates the domestic nature of the individual. This man was loyal to true companionship, but he could love but one.

"The line of heart at the base of the fingers, starting at the index finger, signifies marvelous powers of the occult and spiritual intuitions. It also indicates honor, wisdom and tender devotion, and in this case proves one worthy of nature's divinest gifts. His head line turns quickly downward across the line of destiny into the regions of harmony, imi-

tation and romance, showing him to be of a sentimental and impractical nature. The line of life indicated around the base of the thumb, which is clear
and well defined, shows he would have lived to reach
a ripe old age under favorable circumstances. In
the illustration of this hand is shown many fine
lines spraying downward from the life line, which
denotes loss of vitality and mental force. And the
end of the line turning upward to the region of vitality is a fatal sign with serious reverses in health.
From the location and broken line of the face he
appears to have been a person during his life who
had a great deal of trouble and went through many
trying experiences, and who could not rely upon
friends for help, but who had to shape his own
career.

"The most interesting element in the study of
palmistry is that of dates at which important events
in the life of the individual have taken place, or may
be expected to take place. And in the reading of
this hand, to go into all of the events of his past life
would take more than three pages of this paper,
for under favorable conditions he would have lived
to a ripe old age."

CHAPTER XIX.

JOSEPH JEFFERSON IDENTIFIES JOHN WILKES BOOTH.

Being a constant attendant at the theaters at El Reno, Enid, Oklahoma City and Guthrie in the early part of December, 1900, Booth was much struck by the genius of the leading lady of one of the companies then playing in these towns, beginning at Enid. In fact, Booth regarded her as a genius and sought an introduction through her manager, claiming at the time to be a correspondent of the Dramatic Mirror of New York, and giving his name as J. L. Harris. This young lady is a woman of the highest type and character, and finally the relation of pupil and instructor was established between them, Booth, the supposed correspondent, going with the company from Enid to El Reno, Guthrie and Oklahoma City for the purpose of coaching, watching and training the young actress after his own peculiar manner of acting. Being satisfied with the capability of this actress Booth, or Harris, as he was known to her, made her a proposition, saying that he (Harris) was writing a play to be put on the stage for the seasons of 1903 and 1904, entitled "A Life Within the Shadow of Sin" (Booth's life), and desired that she, the actress of his choice, should play the leading role in the presentation of this play, and that he himself would take an active part, as manager and actor. This agreement having been reached, preparations were being made in 1902 for the proper staging and putting this play before the American people, but some unforseen occurrence over which neither of them had control rendered it impossible to put the play on for the season of 1903-4. This was learned and understood between them through correspondence, and the matter was then given no further consideration. Mention is made of this fact to show the bent and inclination of George, Booth or Harris, the actor, and as a further incident in the identification of Booth.

Believing that if any living man would recognize John Wilkes Booth from the tintype picture of John St. Helen that man would be Joseph Jefferson, of whom I had heard St. Helen so often speak when discussing the successful peoples of the stage, and I sought this best authority at the first opportune time. Mr. Jefferson, who had known John Wilkes Booth since his boyhood and from the time Booth first went on the stage at the age of seventeen, was in the same stock company with him. Among the members of this company being Mr. Jefferson, Edward Adams and John Wilkes Booth, at the age of seventeen playing Hamlet, Mr. Adams playing Laertes, and Mr. Joseph Jefferson, then being twenty-nine years of age and playing the grave digger. Learning that Mr. Joseph Jefferson was playing in Nashville, Tennessee, and that the next day he would reach Memphis, together with his company for the same purpose, I wired him at Nashville for an interview on his arrival in Memphis, which was accorded me. And as per arrangement I called on Mr. Jefferson at the Gayoso Hotel, in the city of Memphis, on the 14th day of April, 1903, just thirty-eight years to the day from the assassination of President Lincoln. We had a long and most interesting interview, and when I handed Mr.

Jefferson the tintype picture, so often mentioned herein and recogniezd as John Wilkes Booth, he took the picture in his hand, saying:

"This is John Wilkes Booth, if John Wilkes Booth was living when this picture was taken." He continued to hold the picture in his hand and in front of his eyes during the entire interview, which lasted more than two hours. I should not say, and do not mean to convey the idea that Mr. Jefferson kept the picture constantly before his eyes, but that he held it the entire time, making long studied examinations of it during the interview and finally said:

"This, sir, I should say, is John Wilkes Booth, but he is older than when I saw him last. I have not seen him since a short time before he killed President Lincoln, at which time I think he was about twenty-seven years of age." After this Mr. Jefferson gave me the history of John Wilkes Booth, from his boyhood up as well as the history of John Wilkes Booth's entire family. And in this connection as a matter of history I deem it my duty to say that I was impressed with the idea that Mr. Jefferson was by no means surprised to see a picture of John

Wilkes Booth at the age of thirty-eight, and gave expression to no more surprise than to ask, ''Where did you get it?'' My explanation to that inquiry, which was quite extended, was listened to with seeming great interest and approval by Mr. Jefferson.

CHAPTER XX.

JUNIUS BRUTUS BOOTH IDENTIFIES HIS UNCLE, JOHN WILKES BOOTH.

While Mr. Junius Brutus Booth was in the city of Memphis, playing an engagement at the Lyceum Theater in support of Mrs. Brune, I sought an introduction to him, and by pre-arrangement was accorded an interview at my office, which lasted for several hours, being of much interest to myself as well as Mr. Booth. At this meeting, because of my former meeting and friendship for and close association with John St. Helen, I was enabled to recount to him much of the private history of the Booth family, which was enjoyed by Mr. Booth with an interest equalled only by his astonishment.

After conversing with Mr. Booth for some moments I handed him the now famous tintype of John St. Helen and asked him·

"Who is this man?"

Mr. Booth took the picture, held it in his hand several minutes, looked at it critically, walked over to the window to get a better light on it and looked at it long and earnestly, finally to my intense surprise he suddenly exclaimed, wringing his hands in grief and excitement:

"Was my father's confidence in me a lie, and did he indeed. die with the secret that my uncle still lived untold on his lips?"

After several minutes he controlled himself with great effort and said to me:

"This is a picture of my uncle, John Wilkes, Mr. Bates, and the best one of him that I have ever seen. There is much that I want to say to you, many questions I must have answered, but this discovery has so astounded and shocked me that I must leave you now. I want to talk the whole matter over with my wife, who is with me in this city. She will understand me and my feeling in this matter. To have so nearly met my uncle, and to find that he has been dead less than a month is very distressing."

Being again overcome by his feelings, Mr. Booth ended the interview, we separating with the promise to meet again the next morning.

The following morning promptly at the time appointed Mr. Booth walked into my office. We talked long and earnestly. I told him again the story of John St. Helen's long life in the West, of the story he had told me of himself, his crime, and his wanderings. Mr. Booth listened, intensely interested, with excitement and often with tears in his eyes, to the ricital, for the first time hearing the whole story, just twenty-eight days after the self-inflicted death of the uncle whom he had never seen, and had always believed to have been killed years before by Boston Corbett.

After much further conversation Mr. Booth requested me to call a stenographer, that he might furnish me a voluntary statement of identification of the picture as John Wilkes Booth. I called Miss F. Wolf, who took down the following interview, which was signed and delivered to me by Mr. Booth, whom I count it a pleasure and a privilege to have met, and shall remember with great kindness.

MR. BOOTH'S VOLUNTARY STATEMENT OF IDENTIFICATION.

"Mr. F. L. Bates: 'I hand you, Mr. Junius Brutus Booth, a tintype picture which was taken at Glenrose Mills, Hood county, Texas, on or about June, 1877, and which was handed to me by one John St. Helen, as a means of at some future time identifying John Wilkes Booth. Will you kindly examine this picture, and in your own way identify the same?'"

306

"I, Junius Brutus Booth, of the city of Boston, Massachusetts, recognize the likeness of John Wilkes Booth, not only in comparison with other photographs and pictures of said John Wilkes Booth, but I can also trace a strong family resemblance and a likeness to different members of my family in the said tintype.

"I am the oldest son of John Wilkes' brother, Junius Brutus Booth, was born in Boston January 6th, 1868. Those now living having any direct relation to John Wilkes Booth are first, myself and my brother, Syndey Booth, 16 Grammercy Park, New York; Creston Clarke, 16 Grammercy Park, New York; Wilfred Clarke, New York; Dollie Clarke Morgan, Vendome Hotel, New York; Adrienne Clarke, Brighton, England, children of Asia Booth, the sister of John Wilkes. Marion Booth, daughter of Junius Brutus, said John Wilkes' brother, also being my half sister, New York.

"The family of John Wilkes Booth's father, Junius Brutus Booth, the elder, and his wife, Mary Booth, consisted of my father, Junius Brutus Booth the eldest, Rosalie Booth, Asia Booth, Edwin Thomas Booth and Joseph Adrian Booth. Subsequent or prior to my father's birth there was another son, who died in infancy.

"The Clarkes mentioned are connected with John Wilkes Booth by the marriage of his sister, Asia Booth, to John Sleeper Clarke.

(Signed) "JUNIUS BRUTUS BOOTH."

"Witness: F. L. BATES."

"I, a stenographer, wrote the above on the typewriter at the dictation of one signing himself as above, Junius Brutus Booth.

(Signed) "MISS F. WOLF."

"Personally appeared before me, a notary public in and for the county of Shelby and State of Tennessee, Miss F. Wolf, who after being duly sworn, made oath that she was the stenographer who wrote this hereto attached typewritten instrument at the dictation of one who signed himself as above, Junius Brutus Booth.

"Signed at Memphis on this 21st day of February, 1903.

"H. C. SHELTON,

"Notary Public, Shelby County, Tennessee."

Mr. Junius Brutus Booth is the oldest living nephew of John Wilkes Booth.

By the authority of these identifications of the tintype picture of John St. Helen as being that of John Wilkes Booth by his nephew, Junius Brutus Booth, and the late Joseph Jefferson, the veteran actor and the world renowned Rip Van Winkle, supplemented with the evidences contained in this book, I announce it as a physical fact that John Wilkes Booth was not killed on the 26th day of April, 1865, at the Garrett home in Virginia, but that he escaped, spent a roving life in exile, principally in the western part of the United States of America, and died by his own hand, a suicide, at Enid, Oklahoma Territory, on the morning of the 14th day of January, 1903, at the hour of 6:30 o'clock a.m.

And thus the story of the life and fate of John Wilkes Booth, the assassin of President Abraham Lincoln, is told.

FINIS.